SEX
PLAYS

To Alison —
with respect and love —

SEX
PLAYS

ERIC BOGOSIAN

INCLUDES

1+1 AND **SKUNKWEED**

THEATRE COMMUNICATIONS GROUP / NEW YORK / 2013

Sex Plays is published by Theatre Communications Group, Inc., 520 Eighth Avenue, 24th Floor, New York, NY 10018-4156

The publication of *Sex Plays*, by Eric Bogosian, through TCG's Book Program, is made possible in part by the New York State Council on the Arts with the support of Governor Andrew Cuomo and the New York State Legislature.

TCG books are exclusively distributed to the book trade by Consortium Book Sales and Distribution.

LIBRARY OF CONGRESS CATALOGING-IN-PUBLICATION DATA
Bogosian, Eric.
[Plays. Selections]
Sex Plays / Eric Bogosian.—First edition.
pages cm
ISBN 978-1-55936-414-0 (pbk.)
ISBN 978-1-55936-430-0 (ebook)
I. Title.
PS3552.O46A6   2013
812'.54—dc23   2013028171

Book design and composition by Lisa Govan
Cover art and design by John H Howard
Author photo by Monique Carboni

First Edition, September 2013

FOR JO

ACKNOWLEDGMENTS

I would like to thank my brothers and sisters at LAByrinth Theater, Johanna Pfaelzer at New York Stage and Film, and the great gang at the Atlantic Center for the Arts at New Smyrna Beach in Florida.

Special thanks to Terry Nemeth and my editor Kathy Sova at Theatre Communications Group.

Thanks to director Mark Brokaw and the cast of *1+1*: Kelli, Josh and Matt.

Finally, a shout-out to my friend and colleague Nikole Beckwith. Thank you.

CONTENTS

1 + 1

PRODUCTION HISTORY

1 + 1 received its world premiere in a co-production between New York Stage and Film (Johanna Pfaelzer, Artistic Director; Mark Linn-Baker, Max Mayer and Leslie Urdang, Producing Directors) and the Powerhouse Theater (Ed Cheetham, Producing Director) at Vassar College in Poughkeepsie, New York, on July 3, 2008. The production was directed by Mark Brokaw. The scenic design was by Riccardo Hernandez, the costume design was by Mattie Ullrich, the lighting design was by Mary Louise Geiger, the original music and sound design were by Obadiah Eaves; the stage manager was Roy Harris. The cast was:

PHIL	Josh Hamilton
BRIANNE	Kelli Garner
CARL	Matthew Maher

CHARACTERS

PHIL, photographer, thirties
BRIANNE, actress/waitress, twenties
CARL, assistant manager of the Steak & Brew

SETTING

Los Angeles

NOTE

The play was originally produced on a stage with an audience on both sides. Props were kept to a minimum so that the stage was bare most of the time, with actors drifting in and out of scenes as they were needed. Furniture consists of a table and chair that can be used to represent a restaurant table or a desk. Actors bring items in and out as they are needed: a camera with tripod, champagne, a laptop computer, etc. One scene flows into the next.

PROLOGUE

Lights up on a casually well-dressed man in his thirties standing center stage. This is Phil. Phil addresses the audience in a vague British accent.

PHIL: People are predictable. Put a person in a certain situation and they'll usually do the predictable thing. There is an algebra to human interaction. We like to think of ourselves as free, but let's face it, we're not. There's a Yiddish saying: "Mensch tracht, Gott lacht." Man plans, God laughs. God may be laughing, but we're still planning.

That's why we're so fascinated by stories. Why do people do what they do? Why do they make the choices they make? We imagine what it would be like to walk in someone else's shoes. What would I do in that situation? Is there really a choice? The Greeks believed in fate. We believe in psychology.

People want things. So they have agendas. They make plans, and then they take actions to get the things they want. People fear things. So they have anxieties. They make plans, they take actions to avoid the things they fear.

You see a girl in trouble. You think, How did she ever get herself in *that* situation? But deep down, you know. She had to have done something. Right?

You read about a serial killer. You think to yourself, How could someone do that? Could *I* do that? But what were the circumstances? What was the algebra?

Someone does good. Another does bad. Is it all the same? Can you blame someone if you don't know the whole story? Don't know the details? Don't know the *math*?

Is there such a thing as freedom? Is there such a thing as morality? I don't know. I try not to think about it too much.

ACT ONE

SCENE I

Phil finds a seat at a table at the Steak & Brew. He begins to read his newspaper while sipping a beer.
   Brianne enters carrying a tray of food.

BRIANNE *(Sunny)*: Here you go! New York strip, baked with sour cream. Enjoy!

(Brianne places the food on the table.)

PHIL: Lovely.
BRIANNE: How we doing with that Becks?
PHIL: I'm good. Thank you.
BRIANNE *(Sunny, without irony)*: You're welcome! Let me know if you need anything else.

(Brianne turns to go.)

PHIL: Wow!

BRIANNE: I'm sorry, you need something?

PHIL *(Laughing)*: No, no. I just . . .

BRIANNE: Oh, steak sauce!

PHIL: No, no, it's just . . . never mind, I'm being stupid.

BRIANNE: What?! Now you have to tell me!

PHIL: Well, you just said, "You're welcome." And honestly, since moving to Los Angeles, I rarely hear that from anyone. No, wait. I'm lying. That's not it. People say, "You're welcome," but only because they're forced to. Because it's corporate policy. You said it like you meant it.

BRIANNE: And that's funny?

PHIL: No, no! Well, yeah. No. Not funny . . . um . . . no . . . good. It's good.

BRIANNE: Oh. OK. Well, just let me know if you need anything. *(Turns to go)*

PHIL: Listen, sorry. It's been a long day. And I've been dealing with assholes nonstop and honestly, it's just refreshing . . . to . . . uh . . . run into a human being.

BRIANNE: I hear you. People suck.

PHIL: Well, they can be *ugly*. You know? And I say, "Why is everyone being so nasty?" Why not be civilized, right? We're not crabs in a bottle. We're *people*. Each and every one of us. Right?

BRIANNE: Even waitresses.

PHIL: Especially waitresses! Intriguing, beautiful waitresses.

(Beat.)

BRIANNE: Uh-huh . . . Well, where I come from we have this weird habit of saying, "Please," and, "Thank you," and, "You're welcome." Just habit.

PHIL: Where's that?

BRIANNE: What? Oh, Phoenix. Near Phoenix. Then I moved to Seattle for a while, then down here. No one in L.A. is from L.A. are they? You're not, I can tell.

PHIL: Originally from London. Near Hampstead Heath.

BRIANNE: England?

PHIL: Ahhh, you're nice *and* you're worldly.

BRIANNE: I was just telling Carl, my assistant manager, "That guy at table five is *not* American." Just from the way you drank your beer, I could tell.

PHIL: I'm what you call a "resident alien." Which is a bizarre term when you think about it. Like I'm from outer space or something. You know?

BRIANNE: "Resident alien"?

PHIL: Green card?

BRIANNE *(Not getting it)*: Oh, right. *(Getting it:)* Right!

(Uncomfortable pause. Inexplicably, Phil has decided to stop flirting.)

PHIL: You know what? I *will* have some steak sauce if you've got it.

BRIANNE: Sure thing! Coming right up!

(Brianne exits. Phil scans his newspaper. Carl, the assistant manager, passes by, giving Phil the barest glance. Brianne reenters with the steak sauce. Phil is immersed in his paper.)

There you go.

(Brianne hands Phil the bottle. He looks up from the paper and beams.)

PHIL: Thank you!

BRIANNE: You're welcome!

(They both get the joke.)

So what? Lemme guess, you're a producer.

PHIL: Now why on earth would you think that?

BRIANNE: Because that's what guys who are hitting on me always say they are. You know they make small talk and then start

with the, "I'm producing a movie! You should come by for an *audition!* . . . At *my apartment!*"

PHIL: Do people really do that? That's pretty crude . . . well, I'm not a producer. I wasn't hitting on you. If I crossed a line, I'm sorry.

BRIANNE: No, it's cool. I mean. Never mind.

(Embarrassed, Brianne turns to go, but stops herself and returns to Phil.)

See the problem is you can't tell the real producers from the fake producers. They're all sleaze-bags. And because I'm an actress, I mean I moved to L.A. to, you know, *act*, I need to know the difference. Between the real and the fake. You know? I'm sorry. This is a stupid conversation.

PHIL: Not stupid. Interesting. No need to apologize.

BRIANNE: Thanks. So, what *do* you do?

PHIL: Me? I'm . . . just a photographer.

BRIANNE: Like for newspapers?

PHIL: Fashion. You know, those guys you see at the foot of the runways? Snapping like hungry turtles? I used to be one of them. I got worn out. Now I mostly do studio work.

BRIANNE: No shit. Ever been to Paris?

PHIL: Paris, Milan, Berlin. Used to live out of my suitcase. But the business is run by very powerful and petty editors—and freaks—and if you don't give them what they want then . . . Anyway . . . I'm much happier now. Lots of glitz covering up a sordid and depressing business. And it doesn't even pay that well.

BRIANNE: Don't tell me about lousy pay.

PHIL: If I'm gonna bust my ass I want to get paid.

(Carl crosses again.)

CARL: Brianne, when you get a chance, table six wants a refill? And three needs their onion rings.

(Brianne barely acknowledges Carl as he exits.)

PHIL: Listen, you're working, I don't want to get you in trouble.

BRIANNE: Can I ask you your opinion about something?

PHIL: Sure.

BRIANNE: You're a photographer, right? OK. Well, this guy wants to charge me nine hundred bucks for a headshot. Is that cool?

PHIL: Nine hundred! For a headshot?

BRIANNE: He says that's a good price.

PHIL: He better be fucking amazing for nine hundred!

CARL *(Off)*: Brianne!?

BRIANNE *(Ignoring Carl)*: It's a lot isn't it?

PHIL: What's a headshot take, forty-five minutes?

BRIANNE: I don't know. I never did one before.

PHIL: Well, I don't do headshots, specifically. But . . . tell you what . . .

BRIANNE: Yeah?

PHIL: I could. I mean . . . I could.

BRIANNE: Yeah?

PHIL: You don't want me taking your picture. You don't even know me.

BRIANNE: No. I do!

PHIL *(Thinking)*: OK, tell you what. You let me keep some pictures and I'll do it for free.

BRIANNE: No, that's not what I was . . .

PHIL: Seriously. You've got a great look. And I'm putting a new portfolio together. I'm always looking for subjects.

BRIANNE: I don't have a great look.

PHIL: You do!

BRIANNE: You know, don't feel that you have to . . .

PHIL: What?

BRIANNE: I'm just saying . . . I don't want anything for free.

PHIL: It would be a pleasure to shoot you. Or not. Either way, I just thought . . .

CARL *(Off)*: Brianne?

1+1

BRIANNE: Shit. I'm sorry. I'm the one who brought it up, right? Ummmm.

CARL *(Off)*: Bri?

PHIL: Look, I'm running late. Why don't you give me my check and I'll give you this. *(He pulls out a business card, hands it to her)* You can call me tomorrow. Or not. Whatever. I'll be in. We'll work something out. *(Extends his hand)* Phil.

BRIANNE: Brianne. Thanks. Phil.

(Phil leaves money on the table, then exits the restaurant. Brianne busses his plate and beer onto a tray. Carl follows her.)

CARL: Was there a problem?

BRIANNE: No. Table six. Right now. I'm on it.

CARL: Tameka got them. But listen, it's very busy, Brianne.

BRIANNE: Yes. I know that, Carl. Thank you!

CARL: And when it gets busy . . .

BRIANNE: I know, I *know*!

CARL: So, what? That guy bothering you?

BRIANNE: No! We were just talking.

CARL: OK.

BRIANNE: A professional discussion.

CARL: OK.

BRIANNE: No offense, Carl, but I don't give a shit about this job, OK? This job is just, you know, something I have to do while I'm waiting for my life to begin.

CARL: I know. I'm sorry. For, you know, implying otherwise.

BRIANNE: I am a professional, you know?

CARL: I know!

BRIANNE: And that guy, who happens to be from London by the way, so I was right, is a *professional* photographer, who is going to take my headshot for free. You got a problem with that?

CARL: No. Of course not.

(Beat.)

BRIANNE: I'm sorry. I didn't mean to snap at you.

CARL: Brianne, you know I totally support everything you are doing. Some day, I am going to turn on the TV and you will be there and I'm going to say, "I used to work with her."

BRIANNE: I appreciate your support, Carl. God knows I need it.

CARL: Your headshot, huh?

BRIANNE: A headshot for an actor is like ballet slippers for a ballerina.

CARL: When you get them done, could I get one?

BRIANNE: One of my headshots?

CARL: Yeah.

BRIANNE: Why in the world would you want my headshot, Carl?

CARL: Well, I could stick it up on the wall. You know like when famous people eat someplace, they hang their picture up by the cash register, right?

BRIANNE: Carl, first of all, I'm not famous, *yet*. And second of all, I don't want every freak and weirdo who comes in here seeing my picture with my name on it so they can find me and track me down and stalk me and shit. It's bad enough.

CARL: Stalk you?

BRIANNE: I was on La Cienega yesterday at a stoplight and this freak in a convertible rolls up next to me and just starts talking to me? Like he has a right? So I ignore him. Next thing I know he's pulling up next to me at *every* stoplight and just staring at me. Why? Why would a guy do that?

CARL: Because you're great looking?

BRIANNE: What? That gives him the right to fucking follow me? Stare at me like a psycho?

CARL: But maybe he, you know, wanted to meet you?

BRIANNE: Oh, yeah, that's the way I want to meet someone! At a friggin' *stoplight*! Jeez, Carl. He could be a serial killer for all I know.

CARL: Or maybe he's a lonely, nice guy who needs to talk?

BRIANNE: You're weird.

1+1

CARL: I'm just saying . . .

BRIANNE: Do you have any idea how fucked-up it is that a person wants to *talk* to you just because of the way you *look*? I mean, *think* about it, Carl.

CARL: OK. I hear you. But then . . . what's the point of looking good?

BRIANNE: Wow. On the outside, you're intelligent, you're sensitive. But on the inside, you're just like that guy at the stoplight. It's kind of scary. Take this!

(Brianne hands Carl her tray. He exits. Then she pulls out a chair and sits.)

SCENE 2

Phil's downtown loft. Brianne is seated before a backdrop paper. Phil enters with a camera on a tripod. He fiddles with the equipment.

PHIL: Just relax.

BRIANNE: I've had my picture taken before.

PHIL: Right. So just be yourself.

BRIANNE: But I should warn you. I'm not very photogenic.

PHIL: You're joking, right?

BRIANNE: No. You'd never know it by looking at me. But it's true.

PHIL: You've never had your picture taken by a professional.

BRIANNE: Well, he was. He was the guy who takes, you know, the class picture at my high school.

PHIL: The what?

BRIANNE: Never mind. *(Beat)* You ever meet Kate Moss?

PHIL: Many times.

BRIANNE: She must be so beautiful in person.

PHIL: No more beautiful than you. In person.

BRIANNE: Right.

PHIL: Brianne?

BRIANNE: Yes.

PHIL: Turn your body so you're facing the wall? Then turn your head and look right at me. *(Brianne adjusts, doesn't get it exactly right)* Right. Now look at me. Use your eyes. *(She does)* Good. Now chin up a bit. Smile.

BRIANNE: This feels weird.

PHIL: I'll put on some music.

(Phil goes off. Brianne nervously fiddles with her hair. Music. Phil returns, lighting a joint.)

Here you go.

BRIANNE: What?! Now?

PHIL: C'mon. Go with the flow. Relax. I know you have it in you.

BRIANNE: It'll make my eyes red.

PHIL: One puff. To loosen you up.

(Brianne reaches for the joint and smokes it. She laughs.)

BRIANNE: This is weirdness! Much weirdness.

PHIL *(Incredulous)*: Why?

BRIANNE: No, I mean . . .

PHIL: What?

BRIANNE: I don't really know you . . .

PHIL *(Focusing his camera)*: Uh-huh.

BRIANNE: Is this like a date? You and me?

PHIL: What?!!

BRIANNE: Never mind. Forget I said that. God! Brianne, shut up!

PHIL: Hey, it's OK. *(Easy, trying to relax her)* Hi!

BRIANNE *(Trying)*: Hi!

PHIL: Feeling more relaxed now?

BRIANNE: No!

PHIL: Tell me about your acting.

BRIANNE: My acting?

PHIL: You said you were an actress. What sort of plays have you done? Shakespeare? Shaw?

BRIANNE *(Laughs)*: Who's Shaw?

PHIL: Ummm. Well, what did you play? In college . . .

(Phil gets off three shots as Brianne answers.)

BRIANNE: I didn't do plays in college. I dropped out. I mean, I actually didn't go. I was going to go, but then I thought, it's a lot of money for, what, a degree I'll never use? You don't need a degree to be an actor.

PHIL *(Busy, not really listening)*: Uh-huh.

BRIANNE: In high school we did this—oh shit, now I can't remember his name—the guy who wrote, you know, that movie about the two guys and the deaf girl . . .

PHIL: Mamet?

BRIANNE: No. It was a guy who . . . never mind. *(Laughs)* See, I'm stoned!

PHIL: Sam Shepard?

BRIANNE: Never mind. I can't think. You're getting me all confused. *(Laughs again)* They make a deal to . . . like a bet . . . anyway, he wrote a play . . . this guy . . . and it . . . never mind . . .

PHIL: I don't think I saw it.

(Phil brings his face very close to Brianne's. A small moment. He reaches past her to straighten the collar of her blouse. He gently takes the joint from her and puts it out. He picks up his camera.)

You know how you were laughing just then?

BRIANNE: When?

PHIL: Just now.

BRIANNE: I guess . . .

PHIL: Do it again.

BRIANNE: What?

PHIL: Gimme a giggle!

BRIANNE: I can't just laugh like that!

PHIL: Of course you can! You're a "natural born actress," aren't you?

BRIANNE: This is . . . *("ridiculous")*

PHIL: OK, let's approach this from a different direction. You ticklish?

BRIANNE: Yes. Very. Very very.

(Phil feints a move.)

Don't!

PHIL: I will.

BRIANNE: I bite.

PHIL: I bet you do.

(Phil catches her in the side. She is ticklish and laughs.)

BRIANNE: Don't!!

(Phil makes another feint move. Brianne laughs. He snaps her picture. Then Brianne stands and says emphatically:)

STOP!

SCENE 3

The break room at the Steak & Brew. Carl is hanging with Brianne.
She lights a cigarette.

CARL: But you don't feel that way!

BRIANNE: Carl, how do you know how I feel? Since when did
    you become a mind reader?

CARL: Sorry.

BRIANNE: And stop apologizing all the time. It's boring.

CARL: Sorry.

(Beat.)

BRIANNE: Sex . . . sex isn't always about love.

CARL: But it is for most people. That's the way it should be.

BRIANNE: "Should"? Why "should"? Listen, Carl, my mom's
    Catholic, OK? I've been dealing with all that guilt and hell-
    fire stuff my whole life. I don't want to hear about "should."

CARL: No, but I mean sex is an intimate thing. Between two people. It should be respected. It's not just a physical thing. It's emotional, right?

BRIANNE: Sometimes, yes. Sometimes, no. You're totally putting *your* own value system on this.

CARL: But, OK, let's say you fall in love with someone . . .

BRIANNE: Yeah?

CARL: I feel weird talking to you about this.

BRIANNE: Why? Because I'm a woman?

CARL: No, because I'm your boss and it could be, you know, um, the sexual content of our conversation could be, uh, construed as harassment.

BRIANNE: What?!!

CARL: We're supposed to stick to work-related topics.

BRIANNE: Oh come on! I'm having a *conversation* with you, Carl! We're discussing a *point*. And by the way, you're not my "boss." I hate that word. You're my *supervisor. Assistant* supervisor.

CARL: Still, the fact that you are voluntarily having a conversation with me about sexual, um, topics does not mean that it's not sexual harassment. I mean, as sexual harassment is *defined*. If we are going by the rule book, we should not be having this conversation.

BRIANNE: The "rule book"?

CARL: Yes. There's a whole chapter on sexual harassment. It's an important topic.

BRIANNE: I never even saw this rule book! "Rule book."

CARL: I'll get you a copy.

BRIANNE *(Laughs)*: Carl, you are like the most straight-edge person I've ever met.

CARL: I take my job seriously.

BRIANNE: You're weird. You know that, right?

CARL: I'm just trying to . . .

BRIANNE: Well, stop trying . . .

(Beat. Carl doesn't want the conversation to end.)

CARL: You don't think I'm your boss? I mean, technically speaking?

BRIANNE: No, you're not my *boss*. Because you can't make me do anything I don't want to do.

CARL: Right. So we're more like colleagues. Friends.

BRIANNE: Friends? Yeah, I guess so. I dunno, Carl. Back home I had friends. We all partied the night I left. I'll never forget it. We all got drunk. Me and my girlfriends and this guy I was seeing who had this crazy idea I was going to marry him. And do you know what my best friend said to me that night? Did she wish me luck? No. Did she wish me success? No. She said, and I quote, "I love you. Please don't go." When I said I had to go, she said, "That's OK. You'll be back."

CARL: I think of myself as your friend.

BRIANNE: My friends want me to fail. So if you're that kind of friend, I don't need it.

CARL: I don't want you to fail.

BRIANNE: I know, I know. Carl! Take that sad look off your face. You look like you're at a funeral! I know you're on my side. And I appreciate it. You're great. You know I love you.

(Weird silence.)

So, should I fold napkins?

CARL: We still have three minutes on the break.

BRIANNE: Yeah, I'm a bit agitated. Enough break. I'm going back.

CARL: OK.

BRIANNE: Carl . . . Thank you for being there for me. I mean it.

(Brianne stubs out her cigarette.)

SCENE 4

Phil's loft. Phil is huddled over his computer, absorbed in what he's doing. Brianne enters and quietly watches for a few seconds.

BRIANNE: Hi.

(Phil looks up, surprised.)

PHIL: Oh, hi! Come here! I'm very happy with these!
BRIANNE: You are?

(Phil swivels the computer so that she can see. There's a physical intimacy between them. Phil takes this for granted.)

Yeah. They're kind of . . . wow.
PHIL: Let me blow one up for you. *(He clicks on his computer, expanding one of the photos)* Nice, eh.
BRIANNE: That's amazing. You're amazing!

PHIL: Not me, *you*. You look great from every angle.

BRIANNE: They don't look like me.

PHIL: Of course they do! You just don't know what you look like, because you spend too much time looking in the mirror. We don't look like the person in the mirror. At all! We look like what we *emanate*. This is what no one understands about portrait photography. The goal is not to document some physical being, it's to get all of it, the person *and* the charisma.

BRIANNE: So it is you. You did this.

PHIL: Both of us. Together. I'll let you in on a professional secret. Half the game is finding a great subject. I knew as soon as I met you.

BRIANNE: Right.

PHIL: C'mon! Look! Brianne! Look at yourself. Look! Brianne, my God! You're fantastic!

BRIANNE *(Seduced)*: "Charisma"?

PHIL: I may have my faults but I *never* lie, Brianne.

BRIANNE: You're lying now.

PHIL: Never.

(Brianne returns to the photos. Captivated.)

BRIANNE: They do look good.

PHIL: The proof of the pudding is in the eating. *(He grabs a coffee table book of photographs, opens it, showing Brianne a page)* You do great things with your eyes. Check this out. It's the eyes that make the difference.

BRIANNE: She's beautiful.

PHIL: That is Lee Miller. Photographed by her lover, Man Ray. Very beautiful woman.

BRIANNE: Her eyes.

PHIL: She was an amazing woman. Look her up. A great artist in her own right. Check this out. *(He grabs another book and opens it for Brianne)* Her father took this photo of her.

BRIANNE: Her father!? She's naked!

1+1

PHIL: Of course! She had a beautiful body. She took nude photos of herself! *(He tears open another book, and another)* This is Weston.

(Brianne scans the photos.)

See? Amazing, huh?

BRIANNE: Wow. What . . . is that her *leg*?

PHIL: Incredible, huh?

BRIANNE: She's naked, too.

PHIL: Well of course. They're *nudes*, you dummy.

(Phil steps away from Brianne as she scans the books.)

It's very important that I take more pictures of you. And not just headshots and portraits.

BRIANNE: "More"?

PHIL: You're a terrific subject. Something emanates from you. You glow!

BRIANNE *(Incredulous, but digging it)*: Yeah?

PHIL: I've been doing this a long time, Brianne. I've worked very hard at it. It's not been easy. Not easy at all. But once in a while, you find gold.

BRIANNE: "Gold"? Right.

PHIL: I need to capture you, all of you. Posed, not posed. *(Beat)* In the studio. On the street. Dressed up. Casual. In the nude.

BRIANNE: Never in a million years!

PHIL: What?

BRIANNE: I am not posing naked, Phil.

PHIL: Why?

BRIANNE: Duh? It's obvious.

PHIL: Not to me. You're saying "no" to something before you've even considered it.

BRIANNE: I've thought about . . . stuff like that . . . before.

PHIL: Stuff like what? I don't even know what you're talking about. Brianne, you are lovely and there's nothing wrong with that.

BRIANNE: OK, OK . . . whatever. But Phil, it's not that I don't trust you. It's that . . . you know . . . I don't really want naked pictures of me . . . you know . . . out there . . .

PHIL: "Naked pictures"? Brianne!

BRIANNE: Well, I don't.

PHIL: You *have* to let me shoot you again!

BRIANNE: Well, yeah. Sure. Of course.

PHIL: This is what we'll do. We'll take it one step at a time. If there's something that makes you uncomfortable, I won't pursue it.

BRIANNE: But *not* naked. I mean first of all we don't know each other that well, right? Plus, you know what? I'd be very nervous.

PHIL: Part of the job of the photographer is making the subject feel relaxed.

BRIANNE: And how would you relax me this time? Shoot me up with heroin?

PHIL: Only if absolutely necessary.

BRIANNE *(Sarcastic)*: Hah-hah.

PHIL *(Touching her arm)*: Trust me.

(Beat.)

Do you trust me?

BRIANNE: No.

PHIL: No?!!

BRIANNE: You're confusing me.

PHIL: C'mon, it's not that complicated. You're making it into something it's not. Trust me. I'm telling you to trust me.

BRIANNE: Yeah?

(Beat.)

PHIL: You know what? Forget it. It's not that important. We don't have to do any more pictures.

BRIANNE: I'm not saying . . .

1+1

(Phil kisses her. Then he leans back, gauging her reaction.)

PHIL: Hi.

BRIANNE: Hi.

(Brianne kisses him back. They kiss again.)

SCENE 5

The break room at the Steak & Brew. Brianne is on her cell phone.

BRIANNE: OK. OK. I will. Me, too. OK.

> *(She hangs up. Carl has been watching her. Brianne lights a cigarette.)*

I'm on break.

CARL: Are you OK?

BRIANNE: Why does everything have to be so complicated all the time?

CARL: Is that a real question?

BRIANNE: All I want to do is work in my profession.

CARL: You will.

BRIANNE: A headshot isn't enough. I need an agent to send out my headshot.

CARL: Oh, well then . . .

BRIANNE: You know? And then I heard you're supposed to have a manager, too. How am I going to get a manager *and* an agent?

CARL: Well . . . I was just going to say, I got a phone number for you.

BRIANNE: Phone number?

CARL: Of a guy. I was in this coffee shop out at Venice Beach? And he was sitting at the next table reading a script? And we started talking, and it turns out he's a CAA agent. That's a very big talent agency.

BRIANNE: I know what CAA is.

CARL: So I told him about you and how talented you are, and he said that you should call him. *(He hands her a business card)*

BRIANNE *(Sarcastic)*: Great, thanks a lot, Carl.

CARL: I thought you'd be happy.

BRIANNE: You did, huh?

CARL: You just said you need an agent, right?

BRIANNE: Carl, listen to me. There's a right way and a wrong way to do things. And someone like me only gets so many chances. OK? *(She hands the card back to Carl)* I can't just call this guy up because you met him in a coffee shop. It doesn't work that way. Now, see, because you talked about me to this guy, I can't *ever* go to CAA to look for an agent. Ever, never.

CARL: Why?

BRIANNE: Because . . . because I can't. Because . . . look, Carl, I know you're trying to help me, but don't, OK?

CARL: You're gonna be a star some day.

BRIANNE: See, even that. You saying that. Don't say that.

CARL: Why?

BRIANNE: It *jinxes* things, that's why! Don't be stupid, Carl! This isn't a game! Maybe you're happy working this dumb job in this dumb place, being a nobody for the rest of your life, but I'm *not*. I'm serious. I'll do what it takes. I'll make the sacrifices I have to make and take the pain I have to take. It's not some casual thing with me.

CARL: OK.

BRIANNE: You've never been serious about anything.

CARL: Yes I have.

BRIANNE: I'm going to do this. *(She looks at the card again)* If I call this guy, I won't even get past his assistant.

CARL: You want me to call him for you?

BRIANNE: NO! Jesus, Carl! Wow. Between you and my boyfriend, I don't know who's a bigger headache.

CARL: "Boyfriend"?

BRIANNE: Whatever he is. That guy. Phil. Fuck. OK. I will figure this out. Everything. I can do this.

CARL: You can.

BRIANNE: Don't help me anymore, OK?

CARL: OK.

BRIANNE: I love you, Carl, but really, don't.

CARL: OK. I promise I will never help you again.

BRIANNE: Good.

(Brianne walks off. Carl follows.)

SCENE 6

Phil's loft. Phil enters, rolling a joint. His camera is set up facing an empty chair.

PHIL *(Shouting off)*: Brianne?
BRIANNE *(Off)*: Yeah?
PHIL *(Shouting off)*: You OK? You ready to shoot some more?
BRIANNE *(Off)*: What?

> *(Phil lights the joint.)*

PHIL *(Shouting off)*: I said are you OK?
BRIANNE *(Off)*: Just a minute!
PHIL *(Shouting off)*: That wasn't so bad, was it?

> *(Phil waits for an answer. No answer. Beat. He takes a step, ready to go get her, then thinks better of it. He returns to his camera, checks it.)*

Fuck.

(He smokes nervously.)

(Shouting off) Bri?!

(Brianne appears. She's wrapped in a white robe, barefoot.)

Hi.

BRIANNE: Hi.

PHIL: Ready to shoot a bit more?

BRIANNE: Sure.

PHIL: Oh, because . . .

BRIANNE: No, I just had to . . . you know, pee.

PHIL: Oh.

(Phil passes the joint to Brianne. She takes it absentmindedly.)

I was going to say . . .

BRIANNE: What?

PHIL: That wasn't so bad, was it?

BRIANNE: No. It was fun. Exciting.

PHIL: You look great. Pictures are going to be very good.

BRIANNE: Cool.

PHIL: Light's important and I got it just right. It's the whole thing, really. Have to balance light, stock, skin tone. It's an art. And I'm good at it.

BRIANNE: Skin tone.

PHIL: OK, if you're paparazzi, that's one thing. But to get the foreground, background, the *sense* of the thing perfect, it takes skill.

(Brianne smokes the joint.)

BRIANNE: I pretended I was playing a part.

PHIL: What?

BRIANNE: Like acting. For the camera. Pretending.

1+1

PHIL: Absolutely. That's it. If there's no spirit, you've got nothing. The inner vitality, that reaches out. It takes two to tango. You send out the spirit and I catch it with my camera.

BRIANNE: So, you're saying what we're doing is like, spiritual?

PHIL: We're making art, Brianne. And you are my muse.

BRIANNE: "Muse"?

PHIL: The muses were like the goddesses of art. They inspired the great artists. That's what you'll be to me. You know?

(Brianne laughs, a little stoned.)

BRIANNE: Phil . . . You are so full of shit!

PHIL: I'm not!

BRIANNE: Yes you are. But it's OK. I like it.

PHIL: I know you do.

BRIANNE: I like you.

PHIL: I like you. A lot.

BRIANNE: Are you going to be *my* muse?

(Phil busies himself with his camera, getting ready to shoot again.)

PHIL: Why do you need a muse?

BRIANNE: For artistic inspiration.

PHIL: How are you an artist?

BRIANNE: Actors are artists. My art is acting and I need to make it.

PHIL: You will. You will.

BRIANNE: No really, I need to. I didn't come to L.A. to waitress at a Steak & Brew!

PHIL: Why don't you take some classes?

BRIANNE: I don't need classes. I need an *audition*. I haven't had one since I got here.

PHIL: You haven't been here that long.

BRIANNE: Look, I think, what we're doing is, you know, cool, and it's something that you and I are doing and I like it a lot. You know that. It's just . . . I came here with a plan, you know? I had a plan and I was going to do my plan and it's just not going the way I hoped it would go. My plan.

PHIL: Maybe you need to adjust your plan.

BRIANNE: You don't get what I'm saying.

PHIL: Maybe you need to take your hands off the steering wheel for a minute and see what happens.

BRIANNE: Is that what you're doing?

PHIL: Maybe.

BRIANNE: You're not.

PHIL: Isn't it all about trying to stay in control? Isn't it all about right and wrong and good and bad? You say you hate your mom. But you know who God is? Your mom in your head. Why don't you do what feels right, instead of what you think you *should* do all the time.

BRIANNE: What feels right?

PHIL: Don't be afraid to let go. Jump into the unknown.

(Phil focuses his camera on Brianne.)

Wait, turn around. But keep looking at me.

(Brianne turns her back on Phil, but turns to look at him. He snaps her photo. Then he begins to walk around her, taking photos at a fast pace.)

Sit down. On the floor.

(Brianne sits on the floor.)

Let go of the front of your robe.
   Open it.

(She does. He snaps her picture.)

Look up at me.

(Click.)

Amazing. Brilliant. Now *look* at me.

BRIANNE: I am looking at you.

PHIL: No, really look at me. With your heart. With your soul.

(Brianne looks up at Phil. He gives her a quick kiss and keeps shooting.)

Look at me as if you love me. Really love me. *(Click)* You are so beautiful. *(Click)* My God.

SCENE 7

Carl's room. Carl is staring at his laptop intently, his headphones plugged in.

CARL: Hi, uh, Marketa. That's a great name, Marketa. What is it, Dutch? Oh. Cool. [. . .] It's Nick. Nicholas. My friends call me Nick. What time is it over there? Yeah, I guess that would be right. [. . .] Just got home from work. [. . .] Uh, I'm a computer programmer. Yeah, I work for Apple. Ever hear of the iPhone? Yeah, I invented the software. [. . .] Oh, no, you don't have to take your clothes off. No. I um, that would make me uncomfortable. I just [. . .] no I understand this is an erotic site. But um, I just want to talk. Can we talk? [. . .] I don't know, about you? How did you end up doing this for a living? [. . .] Uh-huh, uh-huh, now see that's interesting, because who would think that a fashion model would want to be an online escort? [. . .] Yeah, I guess that makes sense. Money is a great motivator. [. . .] Huh? Oh yeah, tons. A lot. Well, you know,

Apple is very successful. Do you have Apple computers in Holland? [. . .] Oh. Well, see, they're everywhere. *(Beat)* You're very pretty. Have you ever thought of visiting the United States? [. . .] Los Angeles. It's nice here and . . . Shit! SHIT! Hello? Marketa? I lost the connection, wait a second. Fucking Time Warner, fuck fuck fuck!!!!

(Carl tears off his headphones. He tries to reconnect.)

C'mon! C'mon! I've lost her. Forever. Marketa! Where are you? Come back!

(No luck. He angrily shuts off his computer and throws it.)

I'm fucked-up. I'm fucked-up. I'm fucked-up. Fuckin' loser. I'm a loser. A fucked-up loser. Why bother? Why bother?

(He storms out.)

SCENE 8

Phil's loft. He enters with a sheaf of eight-by-ten photos. He begins to arrange them on the floor, so he can scan them all at once. Brianne enters. Phil continues to do what he's doing, talking as he goes.

PHIL: When I was a kid, I was an ugly duckling. Grotesque. All nose and chin. I'd ask girls out, they'd laugh at me. That's why I love beauty.

BRIANNE: I don't believe you. You were never ugly.

PHIL: Had zero confidence. Was resigned to spending my life alone, unloved.

BRIANNE: Right.

PHIL: I learned how to use an SLR. I discovered that people love to have their picture taken. I became popular because of my camera. These are really great, Bri. You're getting very good at this.

BRIANNE: Phil?

PHIL: Um-hmmmmmm?

BRIANNE: Where are the other pictures?

PHIL: On the computer.

BRIANNE: Can I see them, please?

(Phil opens his computer, taps in some commands, shows Brianne.)

PHIL: They are extraordinary.

BRIANNE: They are.

PHIL: The light on your skin. Fantastic.

BRIANNE: Phil?

PHIL: Look at your eyes! . . .

BRIANNE: Phil, forget my eyes, look at my . . .

PHIL: You don't like them.

BRIANNE: Phil, you can see my . . . you can see everything.

PHIL: Because everything about you is beautiful.

BRIANNE: I'm seeing parts of my body I've never seen before.

PHIL: You are like Venus. Perfect.

BRIANNE: Venus didn't spread her legs.

PHIL: Stop being so dramatic! Listen, Brianne.

(Brianne is absorbed, looking at the photos, not hearing him.)

Brianne . . .

BRIANNE: What?

PHIL: I have to tell you something. Please listen carefully. I showed the photos to a colleague.

BRIANNE: Colleague? What colleague? Who?

PHIL: A photo editor I respect very very much.

BRIANNE: Oh. I thought . . . you said these were for you only.

PHIL: I couldn't keep them to myself. They're too good.

BRIANNE: You promised.

PHIL: Wait. I see. You don't like them.

BRIANNE: I didn't say that.

PHIL: I've never done such good work. I was proud of what I did. What *we* did. So I had to show them. I'm sorry . . .

(Beat.)

And I'm sorry you don't like them.

BRIANNE: I didn't say I didn't like them. Obviously, they're . . . really something.

PHIL: Let me just tell you Marty's response.

BRIANNE: "Marty"? You showed these photos to a someone called "Marty"?

PHIL: Stop. You're being silly.

BRIANNE: OK. OK. What? What did Marty the photo editor say?

(Brianne won't look up from the photos.)

PHIL: He was knocked out.

BRIANNE: Did you actually give them to him? Does he have them now?

PHIL: That's the not the point, Brianne. The point is that this man is my colleague and he has never been so complimentary of either my work or any subject I have ever shot.

BRIANNE: Phil, please stop bullshitting me.

PHIL: I'm not.

BRIANNE: Look . . . if I didn't know they were me, I would like them, I guess. I dunno. I don't usually look at pictures of naked girls, with everything, um, showing. I mean, these are beautiful in their own way, I get that, I do. It's just . . . I come from a very conservative family. If my mother ever saw these, she'd have a heart attack.

PHIL: C'mon, Brianne! Who am I talking to here? You or your mother? You left home. You live in Los Angeles. You're you. What does your mother have to do with it? Don't you have an objective eye? Can't you see how great these are?

BRIANNE: I said I did. I get it. They're beautiful. But they're also me.

PHIL: Of course they're you. That's the whole point. You are amazing. Check out that expression in your eyes. Do you have any idea how hard that is to do?

1
+
1

BRIANNE: No one's going to be looking at my *eyes*.

PHIL: OK. OK. No one ever has to see these. They will remain private. Yours and mine. It's as if they never existed.

BRIANNE: It's stupid to say that. You already showed them to someone.

PHIL: Marty is totally trustworthy.

BRIANNE: "Marty."

PHIL: I will tell him not to post them.

BRIANNE: Post them? Post them? When did that come up?

PHIL: He asked me if he could post them on his site.

BRIANNE: Oh Jesus. No.

PHIL: Look, his job is to find the best stuff. It's what he does. He said these shots were the best he'd seen in years.

BRIANNE: Phil, I am *naked* in these pictures. Don't you get that?

PHIL: Brianne, for God's sake! What is wrong with you? Will you stop being such a fucking puritan! What year is this? 1899? You are a beautiful woman. These are amazing photographs.

BRIANNE: Don't yell at me.

PHIL: Well, I have to yell if I'm going to get through to you! My God. You know, this isn't just about you and what *you* want. This is about *me*, too. *My* work. *My* career. But you don't care about that.

BRIANNE: Your work is great.

PHIL: Really? Because I would never know that from the way you're acting.

BRIANNE: That's not fair.

PHIL: Fair? What's fair? That I work my ass off for fifteen years, killing myself to perfect my craft, and now, now that I have made something that is brilliant, truly brilliant, I can't show it? I am denied? I thought you cared about me, about what I do.

BRIANNE: This website . . . it's a porn site?

PHIL: *No!* It's a *photography* site. Very serious. Very high end. Photographs of women, yes. Nude, yes. Mostly nude. But only the most beautiful women by the world's *top* photographers.

(Brianne chooses her words carefully.)

BRIANNE: I love your pictures, don't say that I don't. *(Beat)* This is really important to you, I know.

PHIL: It should be important to *you*, too. It *is* you. It's you *and* me, something we're doing together.

(Beat.)

Plus, there's one other consideration.

BRIANNE: Yeah? What's that?

PHIL: You will be paid. For the use.

BRIANNE: Use?

PHIL: People click onto your image, Marty's server registers it, the site pays. Two cents. Every time someone clicks. Every picture.

BRIANNE: Two cents?

PHIL: He cuts a check twice a month.

BRIANNE: A check. For what? Fifty cents?

PHIL: A bit more than that. You want to work in the Steak & Brew the rest of your life?

BRIANNE: You're nuts!

PHIL: True.

BRIANNE: How much do we get? Realistically?

PHIL: Two cents plus two cents plus two cents plus two cents. It adds up.

BRIANNE: Can I think about it?

(Phil takes Brianne in his arms and kisses her.)

PHIL: This will be good. You'll see. You'll thank me.

SCENE 9

Brianne and Carl are in the middle of one of their break-time discussions.

CARL: That I went over to help? Because they were harassing those girls! I mean these guys were complete assholes, and then next thing I know, I'm in the middle of it and the girls are like, "It's OK. We're OK." Right? I'm trying to help and they're like, "Don't bother us."

BRIANNE: Right.

CARL: It's my responsibility to make sure the patrons aren't bothered. I'm *helping* them.

BRIANNE: Right.

CARL: See what I'm saying?

BRIANNE: Yeah . . .

(Beat.)

So what's that got to do with what I was saying about my relationship with Phil?

CARL: Well, empathy. You know? A relationship should be based on people being there for each other.

BRIANNE: Phil's there for me. He's the most empathetic person I know. But at the same time he's very serious about his work. Very serious. I want to be there for *him*. Help him succeed.

CARL: Is he helping *you* succeed?

BRIANNE: What's that supposed to mean?

CARL: What's he doing to support your work?

BRIANNE: Hey, Carl, I don't like where you're going with this.

CARL: I'm just saying . . .

BRIANNE: No. Don't go there. I know what you're doing. You're jealous of Phil. So you want me to distrust him.

CARL: I didn't say that.

BRIANNE: He can't make me do anything I don't want to do.

CARL: OK. I don't even know what you're talking about.

BRIANNE: You know what I'm talking about. You wish you were in his shoes.

CARL: I'm just trying to be your friend.

BRIANNE: Let's forget about Phil. I'm sorry I brought him up. He's just a person I'm working with.

CARL: Oh.

BRIANNE: See, he *is* helping me.

CARL: Good.

BRIANNE: With furthering my career.

CARL: Good.

BRIANNE: Don't get all sarcastic on me, Carl.

CARL: Brianne, I'm not being sarcastic.

BRIANNE: I hear your tone.

CARL: What tone?!!

BRIANNE: I respect you, Carl. But do *not* judge me.

CARL: OK.

BRIANNE: OK.

CARL: OK.

SCENE 10

Brianne and Phil in his loft. Phil enters, uncorking a bottle of champagne.

PHIL: We are celebrating!

BRIANNE: What are we celebrating?

PHIL: The success of the posting. We are getting literally hundreds of thousands of hits.

BRIANNE: Really?

PHIL: Check it out.

> *(Phil shows Brianne a check as he pours a glass of champagne for her, then drinks from the bottle.)*

BRIANNE: Does that say "sixteen thousand dollars"?

PHIL: Two cents times a two hundred thousand viewers clicking on your photos an average of four times comes to sixteen thousand dollars. And that's the *second* check. I cashed the first already.

(Phil pulls out a wad of big bills.)

How many thousands would you like? Two, three?

(Phil peels off some cash and hands it to Brianne.)

BRIANNE: You should keep some.
PHIL: Don't worry about me.

(Brianne stares at the cash in her hand, sipping her champagne.)

Toss it up into the air.
BRIANNE: What?
PHIL: Toss it. It's a nice feeling.

(Brianne throws the cash in the air. They laugh.)

More champagne, my dear?

(They drink from the bottle. The froth makes a mess.)

Two cents plus two cents plus two cents.
BRIANNE: Yeah . . .
PHIL: FUCKING THOUSANDS!!!

(More laughing and drinking.)

Marty wants more pictures. You're a big hit.
BRIANNE: But only for Europe, right?
PHIL: Why? You think your mom's gonna be surfing the net and
    see your naked bum?
BRIANNE: Not just my mom!
PHIL: Hi Mom!!!
BRIANNE: Are you drunk?
PHIL: That's the thing about the internet. It's so fucking huge,
    it's automatically anonymous. Even if someone saw you on

1+1

the street two minutes after they clicked you on a website, they wouldn't be able to put it together.

BRIANNE: Just humor me. Phil. Please?

PHIL: People think you're a schoolgirl from *Amsterdam*.

BRIANNE: And where are all these people?

PHIL: Throw in Canada and he gives us a bonus.

BRIANNE: Canada?

PHIL: It's money, Bri. And money is freedom. It lets you do whatever you want. Act. Write. Take pictures.

BRIANNE: I like money. Everyone likes money. Money cuts through the bullshit. Makes things right again.

PHIL: Yes! When you have money, you can say, "Thank you and fuck you!"

BRIANNE: How 'bout if I say, "Fuck you," to Marty?

PHIL: Go ahead. But you should still take the money!

BRIANNE: And fuck you, too.

PHIL: Why me?

(Brianne pouts.)

Why me, Brianne? What did I do?

BRIANNE: I don't know.

PHIL: Don't fight money. Money makes you free.

BRIANNE: Money is good. Right?

PHIL: Money *is* good. Money is *very* good.

BRIANNE: I like money.

PHIL: I love money.

BRIANNE: Me, too.

PHIL: I love it almost as much as I love you.

(They kiss.)

SCENE II

Brianne and Carl talking.

BRIANNE: I don't have to give you my reasons.

CARL: I'm just curious.

BRIANNE: Why?

CARL: Because I uh . . . care about you.

BRIANNE: See, Carl, you say shit like that and you creep me out.

CARL: Well, also, um, you're a very valued employee. You'll be hard to replace.

BRIANNE: OK. OK. I'll answer you if you promise you'll drop the subject. I'm going to do something else that pays like so much more money it's ridiculous. And money is freedom. It's going to give me way more free time for my acting career.

CARL: If you need more free time I'll put you on half shifts!

BRIANNE: Carl, I can't live on half shifts, OK? I need to make *money*. I stay here and what, I'm gonna be a waitress for the rest of my life, so burnt out I can't audition? No. No fucking way. I didn't come all the way out to Los Angeles so

I could do the same stupid job I could be doing in Phoenix. And you can't make me. I will be an actress and I'm going to do what it takes.

CARL: OK. Don't get angry! I get it.

BRIANNE: You'll find someone else who's good.

CARL: This new job, is it like a show business job? Is that it?

BRIANNE: It's, you know, in the entertainment field.

CARL: It's not dancing is it?

BRIANNE: "Dancing"?

CARL: Some of our waitresses become dancers.

BRIANNE: You know what? Shut up! Wow. You are such an asshole!

CARL: I'm sorry. I don't know what made me come up with that.

BRIANNE: Carl! What do you think of me? God! Is that a fantasy of yours? Me, stripping?

CARL: No! I'm sorry. I'm sorry. I'm sorry. Don't be mad.

BRIANNE: Look. I'll stop by once in a while and say hi? OK?

CARL: Promise?

BRIANNE: Yes.

CARL: Good. That's good. Because, you know, Brianne, it's not just about the job, I mean, now that you're not going to be here anymore, I want to be really honest about how I feel.

BRIANNE: Carl, don't do this. Please?

CARL: OK. I. Look . . . if the other job doesn't work out, call me here. You can always come back. OK? Or whatever. If you need anything. OK?

BRIANNE: Sure. But it *is* going to work out and then my acting is going to work out. And then I won't have to do anything I don't want to do.

CARL: Right. Everything is going to work out. I know it will.

BRIANNE: But only if I really want it.

CARL: I believe in you, Brianne.

BRIANNE: Thank you, Carl. *(Beat)* So uh . . . bye, I guess.

CARL: Well, not permanent "bye."

(Awkward hug.)

SCENE 12

Phil's loft. Loud music. Phil and Brianne are sitting on the floor, each surfing the net on their own laptops. Brianne is wearing an oversized T-shirt over a bra and panties.

BRIANNE: I like the set with the sweater. I don't like the set with the shaving cream.

PHIL: People love shaving cream.

BRIANNE: It looks stupid.

PHIL: Adolescent.

BRIANNE: That's not my point. I don't look pretty. I should always look pretty in the pictures.

(Phil reaches over to Brianne's laptop and presses a button.)

PHIL: Deleted.

BRIANNE: But I love the ones with the sweater.

PHIL: They're going to start a fan club for you.

BRIANNE: In all the prisons.

PHIL: Funny.

(Phil packs a crack pipe, takes a hit and passes it to Brianne. She inhales and coughs. He turns the music up even more loud. They both laugh.)

BRIANNE: Oh, my fucking God!

PHIL: Yeah! How crazy is this shit?

BRIANNE: This has to be the last time.

PHIL: Absolutely.

BRIANNE: *Really*, Phil.

PHIL: OK. But it's not a problem. Why don't we deal with it when it's a problem. It's not like we don't have the money.

(Brianne shows Phil her choices on the contact sheets.)

BRIANNE: These six. But not this one. I hate this one.

PHIL: But you look so vulnerable there.

BRIANNE: I look like a dork.

PHIL: One more? *(Indicating the crack)*

BRIANNE: We are so nuts! I can't believe you bought *crack*!

PHIL: Why? Are you afraid you're going to become ADDICTED?

BRIANNE: People do get addicted. Isn't that why it's illegal?

PHIL: You know who becomes addicted? Losers, that's who. Poor, fucked-up people. Not us. This is L.A., you think we're the only successful people smoking drugs? No. What do you think they do up in those mansions? The whole *point* of being successful is to do whatever the fuck you want. To be free. To buy whatever you want, fuck whoever you want, smoke whatever you want.

BRIANNE: I like this shit! A lot! I could see getting addicted.

PHIL: I'm not saying smoke crack 'round the clock. That would be stupid. But once in a while, when you're relaxing, why not? Connects the fucking dots. You know what I'm saying?

BRIANNE: Sure does. More?

PHIL: All you want.

(They smoke. They entwine into one another.)

You know, not everyone gets to have this.

BRIANNE: This?

PHIL: We love our work. People love us. And we have money. We are on top of the world.

BRIANNE: Yes.

PHIL: You know why?

BRIANNE: We're lucky?

PHIL: No. You *make* your fuckin' luck. The world is full of stupid fucking people. And you make your luck. With your brains, with your skill, with your ass. Life's a problem, you fucking solve it. It's just math. But you have to have the balls to do the math. One plus one.

BRIANNE: Equals two.

PHIL: That's right.

(Phil fills her pipe and lights it up. He watches her smoke. He caresses her. Then he takes the pipe and kisses her. They fall back into a passionate embrace. Twilight darkness envelopes them, the loud music swells.

Time passes. Phil is gone. Brianne grabs the pipe. She sits cross-legged on the floor, smoking, getting into the music. She rocks herself gently as she smokes.)

SCENE 13

Brianne remains in a dim light, smoking. Lights on Carl as he dials his cell phone. Brianne's phone rings. She answers it.

CARL: Brianne?

BRIANNE: Yeah?

CARL: It's Carl.

BRIANNE: Oh, hi.

CARL: What's up?

BRIANNE: Nothing.

CARL: Just called because I was wondering . . .

BRIANNE: How are you, Carl? How're the onion rings going?

CARL: Good, good. How are you?

BRIANNE: Great.

CARL: Working?

BRIANNE: Oh yeah. Lots.

CARL: That's wonderful.

BRIANNE: Lots and lots.

CARL: Anything I might be seeing . . . ?

BRIANNE: What?

CARL: Anything, you know, *Law & Order* or something?

BRIANNE: Oh, uh, no.

CARL: Oh.

BRIANNE: Going to a lot of parties. Networking. You know.

CARL: Right. That's good. You have to do that.

BRIANNE: Meeting people.

CARL: Right.

BRIANNE: How are you?

CARL: You know, same old same old. We miss you.

BRIANNE: I bet.

CARL: You should drop by.

BRIANNE: Yeah? Carl . . . ?

CARL: What?

BRIANNE: Nothing.

CARL: What?

BRIANNE: It's stupid.

CARL: No, it isn't. What?

BRIANNE: I've been so busy, you know?

CARL: Sure.

BRIANNE: I want to stop by. See you. See Tameka.

CARL: You should. Hey, guess what? Tameka got engaged to her girlfriend.

BRIANNE: Really?

CARL: Yeah, isn't that great?

BRIANNE: Yeah . . . uh . . . Carl?

CARL: Uh-huh.

BRIANNE: You're smart. Can I ask you a question?

CARL: Sure.

BRIANNE: Did you ever do something so bad you couldn't tell anyone about it?

CARL: Is this a hypothetical question?

BRIANNE: "Hypothetical"?

CARL: You want me to tell you what I did?

1+1

BRIANNE: No. But . . . uh . . . you did do something, right?

CARL: Why are you asking me this? Did someone say something to you?

BRIANNE: About what?

CARL: I'm just . . .

BRIANNE: No it's stupid to ask you this, because you're a nice guy and you know what you think is right.

CARL: No I don't. I mean, I do. Sort of. But I get confused sometimes. You know, we all have our days, but uh . . . what are we talking about?

(Brianne laughs.)

Brianne?

BRIANNE: You're cute, you know that?

CARL: What did you just say?

BRIANNE: I miss you.

CARL: I miss you, too.

BRIANNE: (————)

CARL: Brianne?

BRIANNE: I'm here.

CARL: Maybe we should, you know, have coffee? You want to have coffee sometime?

BRIANNE: What?

CARL: You want to have coffee one time? You and me?

BRIANNE: How 'bout right now? How 'bout you come over right now and you know we just . . . go . . . somewhere . . . anywhere. You rescue me.

CARL: I'm . . . uh . . . I'm at work right now. I'm closing tonight. And I'm opening tomorrow. So . . .

BRIANNE: Right.

(Phil enters. He has his camera. He shoots Brianne while she talks.)

CARL: But tomorrow afternoon? Like after four?

BRIANNE: Life is so fucking weird sometimes.

CARL: Yeah. I hear you.

BRIANNE: Carl, I gotta go.

CARL: Oh. OK. Should I call you tomorrow?

BRIANNE: You're so great. I'm so glad you called.

CARL: Me, too.

BRIANNE: See you soon, OK?

CARL: Yeah. OK. Tomorrow?

BRIANNE: Sure why not?

CARL: So it's a date?

BRIANNE: I really gotta go. Be good.

CARL: OK.

BRIANNE: I love you, Carl.

CARL: Yeah, I . . . uh . . . me, too. Bye.

(They hang up. Carl is stunned. The light on him dims.

Brianne stands. She faces Phil, who is videotaping her. She begins to take off her clothes as the lights fade to black.)

ACT TWO

SCENE I

Lights up on Phil on his Blackberry behind a desk. He is wearing a tie, his jacket off. His manner is less wolfish and more sober. His British accent has disappeared. He is on the phone.

PHIL: Yes. That would work. Yes. By early next month. Absolutely. Cool. OK, man. Yeah. I gotta jump. Good. Good. Thanks. All right. OK. Good.

(He hangs up, then he checks his watch, calling offstage:)

Traci? When my two o'clock arrives, would you send her right in, please?

(Phil hits auto-dial.)

Hey, honey. How you feeling? Any more kicks this morning? [. . .] Nice. The little guy can't wait to get out. [. . .] I'm done for the day, one more meeting and that's it. *And*

I closed the deal with the guy in Atlanta. [. . .] Oh yeah. Very lucrative. It will pay for the Aruba trip *and* the birthing class. Uh-huh. Uh-huh. Just leave it to daddy.

(Brianne enters. She carries herself in a subdued way. She's older.)

BRIANNE *(Tentative)*: Hello?

(Phil holds up one finger as if to say, "One sec.")

PHIL *(Into phone)*: OK, honey? Listen, my appointment's here, got to run. All right? See you tonight. Let's go to the new Thai place. I'm restless. Me, too. OK. Bye, hon. *(He hangs up)*

BRIANNE: Phil?

PHIL: Hi!

BRIANNE: It *is* you.

PHIL: Uh-huh. Sorry to be so . . .

BRIANNE: When I got the call from . . . what's her name?

PHIL: Traci.

BRIANNE: Traci. Right. I thought, Can't be. But then, you know, there was no other explanation.

PHIL: I was afraid you'd hang up on me, so I had Traci call. I needed to see you face to face.

BRIANNE: Here I am.

PHIL: And here *I* am. *(Beat)* Hey.

(Phil comes around his desk toward Brianne to embrace her.)

BRIANNE: Hey.

(Brianne drifts away from him.)

PHIL: My God! Look at you!

BRIANNE: Look at *you.*

PHIL: Oh right, I'm wearing a tie. Never thought you'd see the day? Well, you can't beat 'em, you join 'em. Funny huh?

BRIANNE: Nice office.

PHIL: They do what they can to keep me happy. I'm a big earner.

BRIANNE: I bet.

PHIL: Wow. Sit down, sit down.

(She doesn't.)

BRIANNE: Can I smoke?

PHIL: Uh, actually, no. We can go out somewhere if you want. Although, I'm not sure where actually, I never leave the office, I think there's a little café and you could smoke out-side . . .

BRIANNE: No, that's OK. I'll just bite my fingernails.

PHIL: You look awesome.

BRIANNE: Do I?

PHIL: The beautiful girl has become the beautiful lady.

BRIANNE: Yeah. You, too.

PHIL: I've become a beautiful lady?

BRIANNE *(Sarcastic)*: Yeah.

(Pause.)

PHIL *(Calling off)*: Traci? No calls. Could you close the outer door? *(To Brianne)* How 'bout coffee? Water?

BRIANNE: I'm OK.

(Silence.)

PHIL: How long has it . . . ?

BRIANNE: Five years.

PHIL: Not five years . . . really?

BRIANNE: Five whole years. And one month.

PHIL: Shit.

BRIANNE: Phil . . .

PHIL: Yes?

BRIANNE: You don't sound like you're from London anymore.

1+1

PHIL: A lot has changed, Brianne. More than you know.

BRIANNE: No but I mean . . . what happened to your accent?

PHIL: Oh that! *(Laughs)* Guess I didn't need it anymore.

BRIANNE: I don't understand.

PHIL: Five years ago, I was a different person . . . I . . . You can't blame me for trying to be something I wasn't. Everyone does that.

BRIANNE: Oh, sure. You don't need something anymore, you get rid of it.

PHIL: Things change. That's all.

BRIANNE: Some things don't change. Ever. Some things are permanent.

PHIL *(Not getting her point)*: I guess . . .

BRIANNE: Like my pictures? They're still out there, floating around the internet. Young naked Brianne.

PHIL: Oh, I know! Isn't that funny? I mean, the last time I looked.

BRIANNE: Last time . . . ?

PHIL: I visit the sites. I even get, uh, royalties every now and then. But you know that, I sent . . . you got the checks I sent?

BRIANNE *(Measured)*: No.

PHIL: Oh, I better be sure I have the right address. I sent them to the old . . . well, we'll straighten it out.

BRIANNE: Can't fucking wait.

PHIL: If you're going to be angry at me, Brianne, this is . . .

BRIANNE: Why would I be angry?

PHIL: I detect anger in your voice.

BRIANNE: I'm happy to see you Phil. Sort of unexpected, this uh, reunion. Got a letter from a brokerage. Call "Traci." Traci sets up an "appointment." All very mysterious. For a minute or two, I thought maybe she was calling to tell me you died or something.

PHIL: That's funny. No, I didn't die. Far from it.

BRIANNE: In traffic sometimes, I'll look around, thinking, Phil might be in one of those cars. Or I'll be filling the tank, you know, just standing there, thinking. And I'll wonder, What if Phil drove up right now? What would I say to him?

PHIL: Well, here I am.

BRIANNE: You never did leave Los Angeles, did you?

PHIL: For a while I lived in Kauai. That's in Hawaii. I met my . . . uh, wife, Janice, there.

BRIANNE: Uh-huh. "Janice." That's a nice name.

PHIL: We've been married three years this, uh, next month.

BRIANNE: Cool. Kids?

PHIL: Not yet. Third trimester. Any day now. A boy.

BRIANNE: Wow. A little boy.

PHIL: Yeah, me with a kid, huh?

BRIANNE: You with a kid. *(Beat)* I'm not angry at you, Phil. Not now. I was.

PHIL: Of course.

BRIANNE: For a long time.

PHIL: Yeah.

BRIANNE: A long, long time.

PHIL: Yeah.

BRIANNE: In fact, it's weird that you found me when you did. Because lately I've been trying to, you know, get on the other side of it. And then, boom, out of the blue, "Traci" calls!

PHIL: Well, yeah. Me, too.

BRIANNE: It was . . . *you* were, a big thing for me.

PHIL: I know. Me . . . me, too.

BRIANNE: You, too, what?

PHIL: I mean to say, you were a big thing for me, too.

BRIANNE: In what way was I a "big thing"?

PHIL: As a relationship, as a person in my life. I mean we were together for almost a year.

BRIANNE: But honestly, Phil, I was just an opportunity, right? Something to take advantage of.

PHIL: It was more than that, Brianne. We were *friends*.

BRIANNE: Were we?

PHIL: C'mon! Of course!

BRIANNE: OK. OK. So I have a question for you. It's a question I really need an answer to. It's been in the back of my mind

1
+
1

for the past five years. How does a friend just disappear the way you did?

PHIL: I had no choice. I was fucked-up. You know I was fucked-up.

BRIANNE: I was fucked-up, too. I didn't run away from *you*.

PHIL: It wasn't *you* I was running away from. It was everything. I owed money to people. Scraping bottom. I had been gambling. And of course, the drugs weren't cheap. So I had borrowed and people were looking for me. I was fucked. Look, we're getting way ahead of ourselves here, the reason I called you was . . .

BRIANNE: I can guess why you called.

PHIL: You can?

BRIANNE: You're probably in some kind of self-improvement program now. I know the drill, I've been to rehabs. You have a sponsor or something and now you're supposed to "make amends."

PHIL: Bri, I'm a coke addict, alcohol addict. Gambler. I didn't know how to handle all the money. I should say I *was* an addict, Brianne. And, this, OK, this is hard to say, I was also a *"sex* addict." Along with a million other things. Dude, I've even quit smoking.

BRIANNE: Don't call me "dude."

PHIL: I'm just *saying*, I understand that now. That I was a total dick. And I was wrong. And it's important that I tell you that I know I was wrong.

BRIANNE: I thought you were an atheist? Isn't all that twelve-step stuff some kind of spiritual thing?

PHIL: I have redefined God for myself.

BRIANNE: Oh, *good*.

PHIL: You're mocking me.

BRIANNE: No. I'm *happy* for you. You're successful, married, a kid is coming. Nice. And now you want to "make amends"?

PHIL: Yes. I do.

BRIANNE: OK. So here I am. Amend away.

(Beat.)

PHIL: I'm sorry. For . . . taking advantage of you. You were innocent. Naive.

BRIANNE: Uh-huh.

PHIL: I should have been more considerate. I should have thought it through, what we were doing. And I should have . . . listen, there were others. Other girls. I'm sorry. I . . . never wanted to hurt you, seriously. Except, honestly, Brianne, I don't know what I would have done differently. I was obsessed with you. Intensely. No, wait, I'm lying. I knew exactly what I was doing. But you have to believe me that I thought what was happening was good for *both* of us. For you especially. You had to get out of that shit job and you made money, right? I really thought it was a good thing. In my own twisted way. I was sick. Can you forgive me?

BRIANNE: I don't blame you for any of that.

PHIL: You don't?

BRIANNE: I was obsessed with you, too. Obviously. And if I didn't want my picture taken, I could have said so. And as far as the others, I knew you were up to something.

PHIL: Yes. That's right! It makes me feel so much better that you see it that way.

BRIANNE: But still, you fucked me over, Phil. You *left*.

PHIL: I was in a bad place.

BRIANNE: We have already covered that part.

PHIL: I had to straighten my shit out.

BRIANNE: (————)

PHIL: You know what I'm saying?

BRIANNE: You *never* checked in on me. You never called to ask me how I was doing. Not one phone call.

PHIL: I wanted to, so many times. And I almost did. But I was such a mess and I was trying to get my shit together. And *(He tears up)* I'm sorry. I'm sorry, Brianne. I never wanted to hurt you.

BRIANNE: You really are sorry?

PHIL: I said I was.

BRIANNE: And you mean this? From the bottom of your heart?

PHIL: Yes!

BRIANNE: Are you crying? You're not crying!

PHIL: Brianne! What do you want me to say?

BRIANNE: Words are cheap.

PHIL: Brianne, you want me to admit I was an asshole, OK, I was an asshole. I was . . . irresponsible. I was . . . sick. But I'm getting better. And I'm allowed that, all right? OK, yes, I made other people suffer. But *I* was suffering, too. So I came to a crossroads and it was either change my ways or fucking *die* . . . And I changed. I . . . did. I have a completely different way of living my life now. And I do live life. Really live it. I don't think about how I look or how much money I have or who I'm fucking. I live my life with love as my most important value, and I know this is going to sound hokey, but I try to be "of service." *(Beat)* And you can be angry. Be angry. I deserve it. But I'm *not* the Phil you met when you were a waitress. I'm not. I'm a new person. I quit the drugs, dropped the bullshit accent, and sold all my cameras. I started over. *(Beat)* And I want to be able to look everyone in the eye and be straight with them and not lie and not hurt anyone. And, you know what? I'm *doing* that. One day at a time. And . . . and I need to make amends. *(Beat)* Make fun of it if you want, but that's what I need to do and that's what I *am* doing. So here we are. And I'm standing before you asking you to . . . let it go.

BRIANNE: And then everything will be all right?

PHIL: No. But better. Than it was.

BRIANNE: And we'll be friends again?

PHIL: Yes. In a way. Not like before.

BRIANNE: Why not "like before"? What's wrong with "before"? Before was good wasn't it?

PHIL: Yes, of course it was good. It was amazing.

BRIANNE: So if it was amazing then, why not now?

PHIL: Jesus, I'm *married* Brianne.

BRIANNE: Your wife, uh, "Janice," wouldn't understand?

PHIL: I seriously doubt it.

BRIANNE: Then you'd have to make amends to her, too.

(Brianne moves close to Phil.)

PHIL: Don't.

BRIANNE: Don't come too close?

PHIL: You know what I'm saying.

BRIANNE: I thought you wanted to make amends?

PHIL: Brianne, look, I still find you very, very attractive.

BRIANNE: Oh, that's good. Because I still find you very, very attractive.

(Brianne seductively touches the collar of Phil's shirt.)

I think about you. Inside me.

PHIL: I think about that . . . too. More than that.

BRIANNE: How perfectly we fit together.

PHIL: We did . . . that. It's true.

BRIANNE: So . . . you still feel that way?

PHIL: Brianne, please sit down.

BRIANNE: Kiss me. Just once.

(Phil says nothing. Brianne leans forward. They kiss. The kiss evolves. Phil breaks it off and walks away.)

That wasn't so bad, was it?

PHIL: Please?

BRIANNE: Touch me.

PHIL: No.

BRIANNE: I thought you wanted to make amends?

PHIL: This is not the way.

BRIANNE: No?

PHIL: You're fucking with me!

1+1

(*Beat.*)

BRIANNE: Did you tell Janice about us?

PHIL: She knows I had another life. That I used cocaine, that I slept around . . .

BRIANNE: "Slept around"! You mean, "pimped"?

PHIL: No. I don't mean that.

BRIANNE: Does she know that you used to shoot porn?

PHIL: It wasn't porn.

BRIANNE: It wasn't?

PHIL: It was adult material.

BRIANNE: Does Janice enjoy "adult material"?

PHIL: No. She's never seen my work.

BRIANNE: Nice girl.

PHIL: Yes. She is.

BRIANNE: OK. OK. But tell me one thing, I have to know, just between you and me, do you come on her face? Do you screw her in the ass?

PHIL: She's not into anal.

BRIANNE: Because I was thinking we could do a threesome! You'd like that, wouldn't you? She could lick me while you take her from behind. That would be good, wouldn't it?

PHIL: You're crazy.

BRIANNE: Did you meet Janice in rehab?

PHIL: I didn't go to rehab. Listen, I don't want to talk about Janice. This isn't about Janice.

BRIANNE: No, this is about wiping the slate clean. Wiping it all away. Wiping me away.

PHIL: Brianne, I have a right to this. I've worked hard to get it all back together. You don't know how hard I worked, Brianne.

BRIANNE: And what do I have a right to, Phil?

PHIL: The same. More.

BRIANNE: Oh yeah?

PHIL: Of course. If you want it badly enough.

BRIANNE: That easy, huh?

PHIL: Not easy. Not easy at all.

BRIANNE: You've been through a lot, huh, Phil?

PHIL: Yes. I have.

BRIANNE: So now that you've apologized and explained what a rat's ass you were, everything's OK again, huh? You can go back to your new life with Janice with a clean conscience. That's the point of all this right? To clean house so you can raise your new family?

PHIL: No.

BRIANNE: Yes.

PHIL: I wanted to make things right with you.

BRIANNE: Me? Me? What do you know or care about me?

PHIL: I care about you.

BRIANNE: Since I walked through that door, you haven't asked me one thing about *my* life. About how *I* am.

PHIL: This whole meeting has caused a lot of anxiety for me. I apologize for being so self-centered.

(Brianne laughs.)

Don't laugh at me.

BRIANNE: Oh, fuck you, Phil! Don't play that Mr. Humble game with me. You always were a piece of shit, you're *still* a piece of shit and you will *always* be a piece of shit. You can "make amends" all fucking day, you're still the most selfish prick I've ever known. Ever.

PHIL: I can't help it if you're still in love with me, Brianne.

(With one long stride, Brianne steps toward Phil and slaps him hard across the face.)

BRIANNE: Shut up! Shut your big fat fucking lying face, you selfish bag of dog shit!

(Brianne backs off, subtly catching her breath, rubbing her hand.)

Asshole!

PHIL: Did you hurt your hand?

BRIANNE: All this "amends stuff"—this is just for *you*. You don't care about me. If I dropped off the face of the earth tomorrow, you'd be so, so happy. You would.

PHIL: This isn't working. Maybe we should call it a day . . .

BRIANNE: No. We're not "calling it a day." We're not calling it a day. We're not done with the *amends*.

(Long beat. Phil tries a cooler tone.)

PHIL: So, what *have* you been doing? Since then. Acting?

BRIANNE: Acting?!!!

PHIL: Your work.

(Brianne laughs.)

BRIANNE: You were always a better actor than me, Phil.

PHIL: Just tell me what you've been doing without the embellishments of resentment.

BRIANNE: Do you want to know? Really want to know? Because it's a lot, Phil. It's a fuck of a lot.

PHIL: I am genuinely curious.

BRIANNE: I bet you are. Because deep down, you're just a little kid with a pack of matches. Aren't you? Lighting fires and watching the pretty flames. Watching everything burn down. And then running away and crying and saying you're sorry.

PHIL: I'm listening.

BRIANNE: Well, let's see. One day, I woke up and my boyfriend was gone. Along with all my connections and my money and my life. I cried. A lot. Tried to figure out what to do. I had no choice. I got clean.

PHIL: Getting clean is hard.

BRIANNE: Don't tell me what's hard!

PHIL: So you're clean? Now? From everything?

BRIANNE: I had a couple of slips. But I'm back.

PHIL: When was the last time you got high?

BRIANNE: That's not important.

PHIL: It is.

BRIANNE: Shut up and listen to me. You left. I got clean. And then I discovered I was pregnant.

PHIL: Shit. Who?

BRIANNE: Who? Who? Who the *fuck* do you think? Who the fuck do you think? Your going-away present to your old girlfriend.

PHIL: That's not possible.

BRIANNE: How do you know what's possible? Those last few months . . . we were barely conscious . . . I couldn't . . . kill it. Her. I thought, I'm such a horrible sinner, I'm gonna kill my baby, too? Anyway, I *wanted* her in my life. I thought this baby will keep me company and help me stay straight. And she did that. *(Holding back tears)* I had to tell my mom. She told me to move back to Arizona. Can you imagine? After all I'd done? To spend the rest of my life in that prison, with my mother watching me, reminding me every day how I ruined my life? Yeah, right. So what was I going to do? Go back to Steak & Brew and waitress? Nah-uh. Live off my photo royalties? They disappeared when you left. And then a solution presented itself. My dealer told me about these "get-togethers." Flat rate. You show up and party with guys and go home with fifteen hundred bucks. No taxes. Cash on the barrelhead.

PHIL: Brianne—

BRIANNE: Oh *yeah*. It started like that. Parties. Hanging out with Hollywood assholes. Then trips to Vegas. "Junkets" they call 'em. And more parties and then straight-up one-on-ones. Some guys really pay the big bucks. The bills got taken care of. My little girl was taken care of.

(Brianne rummages in her pocketbook, removes a photo and shows it to Phil.)

That was taken on her fourth birthday party. Just three months ago. She's beautiful, huh?

PHIL: She's beautiful. Just like her mom.

BRIANNE: No, Phil. *No.* You can't get over on me with this one. This is a *fact.* FACT. That's your biological daughter in that photo. *Yours.*

PHIL: God.

BRIANNE: How you going to "make amends" to *her*, Phil?

PHIL: I will. I promise.

(Brianne blows her nose, cleans up.)

BRIANNE: Yeah? She has to go to school. Everything costs money.

PHIL: So you're still using drugs? Off and on?

BRIANNE: None of your fucking business.

PHIL: Using drugs around this child?

BRIANNE: Shut the fuck up!

PHIL: I will give you some money.

BRIANNE: No not "some" money. *A lot* of money. Every month.

PHIL: Brianne, my means are limited.

BRIANNE: Yeah, I can see that.

PHIL: I have a family of my own.

BRIANNE: This is a paternity situation here, big guy. *Comprende?*

PHIL: What?

BRIANNE: Pa-ter-ni-tee.

PHIL: No. Do not go there.

BRIANNE: Where? Where am I going, Phil? Where am I going that you didn't take me by the hand and lead me to?

PHIL: No one told you to have that baby, Brianne.

BRIANNE: "That baby" is *your* baby. *Your* daughter. Fucker. You didn't even ask me her name. You *fucker.* You piece of shit fucker. I'll take you to court and I'll string you up by your big hairy balls.

PHIL: Oh, fuck this. This is bullshit. You come in here and play the victim. Like everything just "happened" to you. Nothing happened you didn't want to happen. You like things all fucked-up like this, because then you don't have to make decisions. You wanted to be an actress. Why didn't you become an actress? Because you couldn't do what you had to do. It was much easier letting me show up and fuck things up so you could spend the rest of your life being angry at me.

(Beat.)

BRIANNE: You tricked me. You took advantage of me. You fucked me over and left me with a baby to take care of.

PHIL: (———)

BRIANNE: You have to make a decision, Phil. You want me to go? Or do you want me to stay? Or do you wanna make a deal? Because if I walk out that door, you will not be happy about what happens next.

(Beat.)

PHIL: You try to put this on me. But it's *not* me, Bri. It's *you*. You think I didn't know you were on heroin? I knew. Of course I knew. It freaked me out because I thought it was my fault. My whole life I could fix anything I set my mind to. But I couldn't fix this. I was between a rock and a hard place. And . . . and . . . I know you're not going to believe me, but I *loved* you, Bri. So for your own good . . . and mine, I left. We had something, *together*, and that something was over. That's all.

BRIANNE: Not over.

PHIL: Yes. Over then. Over now. I'm sorry.

BRIANNE: Uh-huh? You think . . . you think you can say, "I loved you," and that's what? Gonna change things? No. NO!

PHIL: Wait a minute! Everybody breathe for a second.

BRIANNE: No.

PHIL: Brianne. Listen to yourself. You're being irrational.

BRIANNE: I'll show you irrational.

PHIL: Don't push me into a corner, Bri. Don't.

BRIANNE: You ruined my life! You have to make things right!

PHIL: But money won't do that!

BRIANNE: Fuck you. I will fuck you up.

PHIL: Wait. Wait. Stop. Stop talking. *Think.* You're an *addict.* Bri! Jesus. Come on. Don't threaten me. You don't want to threaten me. You're a *prostitute.* You're still using drugs. I can tell.

BRIANNE: That has nothing . . .

PHIL: You are . . . still . . . using . . . drugs.

BRIANNE: (———)

PHIL: So . . . come on, walk through this with me. You have no money, no resources. You're one step away from being homeless. And I can't fix that. I can't fix *you.* There isn't enough money in the world to do that. I invited you up here today because I wanted to make things right, and you spring all this on me.

BRIANNE: I will go to court.

PHIL: No.

BRIANNE: Yes. I want a major settlement. You wrecked my life, I will wreck yours. *(Beat)* I'll call Janice.

PHIL: Don't say that. You don't wanna say that.

BRIANNE: I will. I will call her. I don't care.

PHIL: You're backing me into a corner here.

BRIANNE: What am I supposed to do, Phil?

PHIL: What am *I* supposed to do? Support a hooker and her kid? I can't do that. I *won't.*

BRIANNE: No. NO! Fuck that. Fuck that! Phil . . . motherfucker!

PHIL *(Adopting a kindly tone)*: Listen, I feel for you, but I have a new family. An unborn son. And I will protect him with everything I can get my hands on, no matter how much I once loved you. And I did love you. And because I loved you, still love you, I'm going to say this once and I'm not going to repeat myself. You have *no* resources. I have *all* the resources. Lawyers. Friends. Friends of friends. *Cops.* People who will stand like a wall of stone between you and me. Like fire.

BRIANNE: You don't know what I can—

PHIL: I offered you some money. And I will make good on that offer. And I made my amends whether you think they're bullshit or not. So, I am not guilty. Uh-uh. I suggest you accept both the cash and the apology. Because if you don't . . . then honestly . . . I feel I don't owe you a thing.

BRIANNE: Phil!

PHIL: No. I'm not paying for what you've done to yourself.

BRIANNE *(Composing herself)*: You're bluffing.

PHIL: You're threatening me. You're forcing me. No. No. I'm sorry. You made this bed. *You.* Not me. It's you who has to lie in it. *(Calling off)* Traci, I'm done for the day.

(Phil hands Brianne a business card.)

This is my lawyer's number. Call him and he will arrange some money. *Don't* call me. I mean it.

(He starts out, then stops.)

(Bemused) You know, it's funny, you were the one who wanted your picture taken. You started this. You're lucky I'm giving you anything at all.

(Brianne stares at the card, then looks at the photograph of her daughter.)

1+1

SCENE 2

Carl enters his apartment, carrying a large Starbucks coffee.

CARL: How did it go?
BRIANNE: All right.
CARL: You sure?
BRIANNE: Yes.

>   *(Beat. Carl puts his coffee down carefully.)*

CARL: He asked you to forgive him?
BRIANNE: Yes.
CARL: Did you show him the picture?
BRIANNE: Yes.
CARL: Did he get upset?
BRIANNE: In a way.
CARL: Is he going to pay you?
BRIANNE: I don't know. Yes. I guess. I don't care.
CARL: You don't *care*?
BRIANNE: He said some things.

CARL: Of course he said some things. That's how he gets what he wants. He's a con-man. *(Beat)* What kind of things?

BRIANNE: He said it was my fault.

CARL: Your fault.

BRIANNE: He said I was, you know, thought of myself as a victim, that I did everything because I wanted to. That I screwed up because I wanted to. That it was all my fault. What happened.

CARL: That's nuts!

BRIANNE: He said he would give me some money. But not what I want. Not enough. Some. Not enough.

CARL: Brianne, this is fucked-up.

BRIANNE: I know.

CARL: I mean, I don't make enough money to keep this situation going. Supporting you and your daughter. I mean, Brianne, what about school? I can't afford that.

BRIANNE: I can go make some money.

CARL: No, you can't do that anymore.

BRIANNE: I'm sorry.

CARL: He owes you!

BRIANNE: I don't know. I guess. Or not. I don't know.

CARL: So where does that leave everything?

BRIANNE: Look, I'll leave if you want. *We'll* leave. You don't have to take care of us. I don't expect you to.

CARL: I don't want you to leave.

(Pause.)

BRIANNE: I appreciate everything you've done, Carl.

CARL: Yeah?

BRIANNE: Yeah.

CARL: Wow, I'm really upset here.

BRIANNE: I know.

CARL: This guy. This guy.

BRIANNE: I know.

CARL: And seeing him again. You seeing him. Did you feel anything. For him?

1+1

BRIANNE: Carl.

CARL: No. Did you?

BRIANNE: Don't.

CARL: You did. Didn't you? Your heart went flippity-flop.

BRIANNE: Stop. I've had a hard enough day!

CARL: Did you kiss him?

BRIANNE: Carl.

CARL: This guy. This *creep*, who did all of this to you and now won't even . . . won't even take care of . . . the mess he's made. On top of that . . . you still have a thing for him. Fuck. And I, here I am, the fucking jerk, cleaning up . . . cleaning up his mess. Fuck.

BRIANNE: Carl, you've been so good to me. To us.

CARL: Fucking chump.

BRIANNE: No. You're not.

CARL: Yes.

(Brianne goes to Carl, gently touching him.)

BRIANNE: I owe you so much. Without you, I would have been so lost. So lost.

CARL: You always say that.

BRIANNE: I mean it.

CARL: Don't start telling me how much you appreciate me.

BRIANNE: But I do!

CARL: Right.

BRIANNE: I do.

CARL: You say it, but you don't mean it.

BRIANNE: I do mean it.

CARL: But not in the way . . .

BRIANNE: What?

CARL: You know what. Never mind.

BRIANNE: Carl.

CARL: If a person has to ask for love, then it's not the same.

BRIANNE: You can ask.

CARL: No. Listen. You stay here. For now. You can stay here.

BRIANNE: Shhhhhhh.

(Beat.)

CARL: You and your daughter mean so much to me.
BRIANNE: I know.
CARL: And I don't mean anything to you.
BRIANNE: That's not true.
CARL: Yes. It is.
BRIANNE *(Caressing him)*: Let me show you.
CARL: Huh?
BRIANNE: Let me show you. How I feel.
CARL: No. *(Long pause)* It's OK. Maybe tomorrow.

*(Carl moves away from her. He picks up his coffee, sips it; his
hand is shaking and he spills coffee on himself.)*

Shit! Man . . . I just bought this . . .

(Brianne rushes to him, tries to wipe the stain.)

BRIANNE: It's OK, it's OK.
CARL *(Angrily)*: It's ruined. Never mind.

(Brianne breaks away from Carl.)

BRIANNE: FUCK!

(Brianne gets out her phone. Dials.)

CARL: Who are you calling?

(Brianne is listening.)

BRIANNE: Hello? Is this Janice? My name is Brianne? I'm a
friend of Phil's? [. . .] Your husband? Phil? [. . .] Philip.

1±1

OK, Philip. Well, I'm a friend of his, I mean, I *used* to be a friend of his, and I think you and I should talk . . . can we meet [. . .] What? [. . .] Yes . . . yes . . . *(Long pause)* Yes, that's right, but we should [. . .] Oh . . . but you don't know . . . you don't [. . .] Oh . . . you're . . . you're . . . no, but listen, you're making a mistake . . . he's . . .

(Looking at the phone) She hung up on me.

CARL: Who was that?

BRIANNE: She said she already knew. That she didn't care . . . That she forgave him.

CARL: You called his wife? You did it? Brianne!

BRIANNE: She said, "I'm not making a mistake, *you* made a mistake." She said that. Bitch. Cunt.

(Brianne dials again. Carl takes the phone from her.)

CARL: No. It's over, Brianne.

BRIANNE: It's *not* over. It's never over. What the fuck do you know? You never wanted anything, never wanted to be anything. I'm not that. I'm not that. Fuck him. No.

(Brianne tries to get the phone from Carl. He pushes her and she falls down.)

You know what? Fuck you, too. Fuck you. Fuck all of you. But especially *you*. Fucking boy scout. You *are* a fucking chump. Fucking boy scout. Fuck you!

CARL: You're upset.

(Carl helps her get back up.)

BRIANNE: No. No. It doesn't work that way, Carl. "Understanding" is bullshit. It's for chumps like you. For suckers. Phil was right. Everything he did was right. That's all. Fuck you. Fuck everybody.

(Brianne storms out. Carl throws his coffee against the wall.)

SCENE 3

Phil sits at a table at the Steak & Brew, reading a paper and nursing a beer.

    Carl walks by Phil's table.

CARL: How's everything this evening?

PHIL: Good, good. Uh . . .

CARL: Sir?

PHIL: Nothing.

CARL: Is something wrong?

PHIL: No . . . I just, I was hoping to run into someone who used to work here.

CARL: Who?

PHIL: What?

CARL: Who was it who used to work here?

PHIL: Her name was Brianne . . . Brianne was her name. Waitress.

CARL: Brianne. That was a while ago.

PHIL: Yes.

CARL: Six years ago.

PHIL: Yes. You know what happened to her?

CARL: Well, gee, she wasn't here very long.

PHIL: But you remember her.

CARL: Oh, sure, I just started here. I manage the place now. Used to work shifts. Now I don't have to do that. I just drop by and keep an eye on things . . . Six years ago . . .

PHIL: Yeah.

CARL: Why you looking for Brianne?

PHIL: Actually, it's funny, I owe her some money. But I lost track of her . . . And anyway, I thought I might find her here.

CARL *(Figuring it out)*: I see.

PHIL: You can't trace her? Find her?

CARL: Brianne?

PHIL: Brianne.

CARL: Uh . . . no. Can't help you there.

(Beat.)

PHIL: Well. Can't say I didn't try. Say, could you ask the waitress to get my check? I'm running late.

CARL *(Sharply)*: Tameka! Check!

(Beat.)

I'm Carl.

(Carl extends his hand. Phil takes it.)

PHIL: Phil.

CARL: She'll be right with you, *Phil*.

PHIL: Thanks.

(Carl doesn't leave Phil's side. Phil ignores Carl.)

CARL: Married?

PHIL: Hmmm? Yeah.

(Beat.)

CARL: Kids?

PHIL: Actually, we just had our first last year.

CARL: Really? That's interesting.

(Carl pulls out his wallet. Flips out a photo.)

My daughter.

(Phil glances at the photo with no great interest.)

PHIL: Pretty.

(Carl watches Phil's reaction.)

CARL: Yeah. She is. She'll be five in December. Great kid.

PHIL: I bet.

CARL: I love her with all my heart.

PHIL: Yeah. I know what you mean.

CARL: Her mom . . . her mom passed away about six months ago.

PHIL *(Heartfelt)*: God, I'm sorry to hear that.

CARL: Yeah. Well. Drugs. You know. Overdose.

PHIL: That's terrible.

CARL: Yeah. But life goes on. At least I have my little girl.

(Pause. Nothing more to say.)

Your waitress will be right over.

(Carl steps away.)

PHIL: Thanks.

CARL: What's that?

PHIL: I just said, "Thanks."

CARL: Oh. You're welcome. Or should I say, "Thank *you*!"?

(Carl walks off. Phil takes a sip from his beer, looks around expectantly.
Blackout.)

END OF PLAY

SKUNKWEED

PRODUCTION HISTORY

Skunkweed was developed as a workshop production at the Atlantic Center for the Arts in New Smyrna Beach, Florida, in fall 2003. The production was directed by the author. The cast was:

JERRY	Josh Lefkowitz
JO-ELLEN	Sarah Utterback
CHET	Gideon Banner
BONER	Beau Allulli
CHRISTINE	Elliotte Crowell
RAINBOW	Nikole Beckwith

CHARACTERS

JERRY, TV writer on location, thirties
JO-ELLEN, local, twenties
CHET, Jo-Ellen's older brother, thirty
BONER, Chet's best friend, twenty-five
CHRISTINE (with her baby Danielle), Chet's wife, thirty-five
RAINBOW, Boner's girlfriend, twenty
ROOM SERVICE WAITERS

SETTING

Florida, just south of Daytona Beach

ACT ONE

Jerry, thirties, enters the somewhat plush hotel room with Jo-Ellen, twenties. Jerry flips on the lights, hangs the "do not disturb" sign on the door. With a big smile, he pulls a beer out of a brown paper bag. Jo-Ellen stands to one side, expectant.

JERRY: Too bright. Let's do this.

> *(Jerry pulls the chain on a floor lamp. Nothing happens. He pulls again. And again. Nothing.)*

Fuck!

> *(Jerry grabs the phone, pushes a button.)*

Hello? Yes. Yeah this is Mr. Goldberg in 1626? Yeah, I called earlier about my lamp? *(Listens)* Right. Yeah. Well, no. Not right now. Tomorrow? OK. I mean, I'm checking out tomorrow. But never mind. Yeah. Yes. I want it. I did want it. But never mind . . . *(To Jo-Ellen)* Maintenance.

JO-ELLEN: Oh.

(Jerry presents Jo-Ellen with a beer.)

JERRY: Want one?

JO-ELLEN: OK.

JERRY: Sit! Sit!

JO-ELLEN: Anywhere?

JERRY: The couch?

(Jo-Ellen perches on the little couch. She checks out the room, curious.)

JO-ELLEN: Big place.

JERRY: They call it a suite.

JO-ELLEN: Uh-huh.

JERRY: This is so . . .

JO-ELLEN: Yeah.

JERRY: This is not the usual thing with me.

JO-ELLEN: No?

JERRY *(Sips beer)*: I'm here, to . . . uh . . . you know, work. Write. I'm a writer. Teleplays, plus working on a novel, that kind of thing. But I convinced them—"the suits," the executives—to fly me down here to do some research on a series pilot for Showtime. I figured I'd look around. Get the feel, you know? Eat some ribs, watch a stock car race. It's good. It's good. But I get, you know, the road, lonely. Stuck in this room. Lots of TV. Room service food. Long days trying to knock out an outline, getting nowhere. Then, I dunno, I went for a ride for some fresh air. And you know. It's weird. I'm married.

JO-ELLEN: Oh.

JERRY: Yeah. In L.A. I'm married. I mean, I'm married here, too, I am a married man. But it's . . . it's very complicated. It's not good. Obviously.

JO-ELLEN: Yeah.

JERRY: You must hear this kind of thing all the time.

JO-ELLEN: Kids?

JERRY: Ummm. No . . . *(More firmly)* No. *(Absolutely sure)* No. *(Beat)* Whew. I'm nervous. This really isn't my MO.

JO-ELLEN: No. Me neither.

JERRY: What's your name again?

JO-ELLEN: Jo-Ellen.

JERRY: Right. And I'm Jerry. How's the beer?

JO-ELLEN: Good. Cold.

JERRY: You want me to put on some music?

JO-ELLEN: OK.

(Jerry fiddles with his laptop computer, some soft Kenny G–type music begins to play.)

JERRY: I carry all my music on my computer. I didn't even know I could do that. Just put it on the computer. On the hard drive. It's amazing really when you think about it. That little hard-drive has *all* my work on it. I mean, *all* my work. Everything I've ever written. And it doesn't take up any space at all. A whole novel. Five screenplays. My address book. Plus the Encyclopedia Britannica. The OED. An Atlas. All in this little flat thing.

JO-ELLEN: You want to sit down?

JERRY: Right. Good idea.

(Jerry sits next to Jo-Ellen, who smiles at him. Jerry smiles back. He sips his beer. She sips hers. Slight thaw. Jerry's cell phone rings.)

Shit. One sec. Sorry. *(Into his phone)* Hello?

(Jerry wanders into the bathroom to talk. While he's on the phone, Jo-Ellen snoops in his briefcase, peeks at the paperwork on the desk.)

Oh, hey, honey. Nothing. Just eating the room service dinner, watching CNN. How're you doin? [. . .] Good. Good. [. . .] Really? How much did that cost? [. . .] No, I'm not saying that, honey, I'm just . . . never mind. No, never mind. So, uh, good. [. . .] Huh? No, well yeah, kind of. Long day. So yeah, tired. A little jetlag, too. [. . .] Yeah. So. OK. I'm gonna get back to uh . . . [. . .] Yeah. Don't want it to get cold. OK. [. . .] Love you, too. 'Night. *(Hangs up, returning to Jo-Ellen)* My wife.

JO-ELLEN: Yeah.

JERRY: Checking up on me.

JO-ELLEN: Uh-huh.

JERRY: Things aren't so good, right now, between us.

JO-ELLEN: I'm sorry.

JERRY: No. I mean. This is stupid, me talking to you about my wife. You of all people.

(Beat.)

JO-ELLEN: Why not?

JERRY: God I'm so nervous.

(Jerry abruptly sits down. He puts his arm around Jo-Ellen's shoulder and kisses her. Then he stops.)

That's a start.

JO-ELLEN: Yeah.

JERRY: Ummm. I don't have any condoms.

JO-ELLEN: Oh.

JERRY: I figured . . . you would. You know. Um. So should we take a shower together?

JO-ELLEN: Wow. Condoms. Showers.

JERRY: Not that I think that you . . . you know . . .

JO-ELLEN: What?

JERRY: Need a shower . . . or a condom . . .

JO-ELLEN: I took a shower this morning.

JERRY: No, I'm sure you did. I'm sure you did.

(Jo-Ellen suddenly grabs a pillow off the couch and hugs it. Jerry gets confused.)

No.

(Big beat. Jerry begins to speak quickly.)

Look, can we just stop for a second and take a little time-out here? Like, OK. I go for a ride to get some fresh air. Stop at a light. And there you are, standing. Right? I'm just driving by, stopped at a red light and you're standing there. And you smile. Right?

JO-ELLEN: Right.

JERRY: So I smile back. So. I mean, you were just standing there. That's like the spot, right? To stand in?

JO-ELLEN: I was waiting for my brother.

JERRY *(Taking this in)*: Right.

JO-ELLEN: He said he'd come by to pick me up and he was late.

JERRY: Right. Your brother.

JO-ELLEN: He works at the Chevy dealership. He's a truck mechanic. Gets off at five.

JERRY: I see. But I mean. I smiled at you, you smiled at me. I rolled down my window and said, "Hey." Then you said, "Hey." Then I said, "What are you doing?" And you said, "Nothing." And then I said, "You want to go for a ride?" And you said, "Where to?" And I said, "My hotel." Right? I said, "My . . . hotel . . ."

JO-ELLEN *(Sunny, but forced)*: And here we are!

JERRY: No, wait, don't get ahead of me here. So I said, "My hotel." And you said, "OK." And, so, you came to my hotel and you came upstairs and like here we are in my suite. You know what I'm saying? You follow my drift? Like you were standing in the street and I asked . . . *(He stops mid-sentence, thinking hard)*

JO-ELLEN (*Trying to follow his logic*): Right . . . ?

(*Beat.*)

JERRY: Your brother works as a mechanic at the Chevy dealership?

JO-ELLEN: Uh-huh.

JERRY: So where is your mechanic brother now?

JO-ELLEN: Beats me. He turned his cell phone off.

JERRY: Right. So. OK. So I guess what I'm getting at is, not
to put too fine a point on it, but umm, how much is this
gonna cost me? We should probably get that figured out
first. Right?

JO-ELLEN: The room?

JERRY: No. You know what I'm saying. Right? You do know?

JO-ELLEN: What?

JERRY: Ummmm. OK. One more time-out. This is . . . I'm
sorry. *I* had the impression . . . And I don't know how to
say this without seeming like a complete jerk, but see, in
Los Angeles when a woman stands in front of a funky motel
and talks to people who are driving by in their cars? Then,
that's kind of, you know, a come-on, like you know, uh, *sex*.

JO-ELLEN: "Sex."

JERRY: Yeah!

JO-ELLEN: You have got to be the most nervy guy I've ever met.

JERRY: No, you don't understand. See I'm *not*. I'm. I'm. Oh shit.
See *I* thought, you were, you know, look, I'm just going to
say it: I thought you were a hooker.

(*Jo-Ellen sips her beer, watching him. Beat.*)

JO-ELLEN: Oh.

JERRY: I'm sorry. I mean if that's not the case. Wow. Or is it? You're
fucking with me, right? Wow. You're not fucking with me.
I knew it. You're too good-looking to be a prostitute.

JO-ELLEN: You thought I was a prostitute?

JERRY: Well, something like that. Yeah.

JO-ELLEN: So you thought . . . Wow. Like you thought I came up here . . . Wow.

JERRY: Yeah. Isn't that funny? *(Laughs)* And you know, I know you won't believe this, but I've never been with a prostitute. Ever. Never. It's just that, you know you smiled at me. *You.* And I guess, I'm not used to pretty women smiling at me, when I drive by. In my car. I mean, never in a million years, would I assume that you were smiling at me, to just you know, *smile* at me.

JO-ELLEN: That's funny.

JERRY: Yeah, see that's what I'm saying!

(They both sip their beers. Beat.)

Look, I guess you should go. I'm sorry. I'll call you a cab.

JO-ELLEN *(Brow furrowed)*: Yeah.

(Before Jo-Ellen can say another word, Jerry picks up the phone, pushes the button for the front desk.)

JERRY: Yes. Hello, could I order a cab? [. . .] No, for right now. [. . .] No, local I think. *(Covers phone, to Jo-Ellen)* Where?

JO-ELLEN: Uh, Mission and Ingram?

JERRY *(To phone)*: Mission and Ingram? [. . .] Right. [. . .] OK. Ten minutes. Thanks. *(Hangs up)* Ten minutes.

JO-ELLEN: OK.

JERRY: So! Well, a funny story to tell somebody some day.

JO-ELLEN: Yeah.

JERRY: So . . . what *do* you do?

JO-ELLEN: Huh?

JERRY: When you're not standing on a street corner waiting for your brother to pick you up. Sorry that wasn't very nice, but I mean what do you do, for a living?

JO-ELLEN: I work at Books-A-Million. I'm a cashier.

JERRY: Right. Well, that's nice. Books. You like books?

JO-ELLEN: Sometimes.

JERRY: I don't blame you. I'm a writer and I hate most of the shit out there.

JO-ELLEN: Oh, there's stuff I like. Did you read *Lovely Bones*?

JERRY: Yeah. That was good. In its way. A little treacly, but yeah, sure.

JO-ELLEN: Wasn't it awesome?

JERRY: Yeah.

JO-ELLEN: It made me think about my own life, you know? From a different perspective? Just, uh, you know, the way we live. Here. My family. I mean, it's good, but it's boring sometimes? But it's just, you wonder like, OK, is this it? And when I die, will that be all there is? *(Beat)* You're a writer, huh?

JERRY: Yeah.

JO-ELLEN: What do you write?

JERRY: Movies. TV. Mostly TV.

JO-ELLEN: Really? What TV?

JERRY: Nothing you would remember. I was on staff at *Lost*, got credit on some original *Law & Order*s. Now I write pilots that don't get made.

JO-ELLEN: You must earn a lot of money.

JERRY: Not really. Well, I mean, compared to, you know, what regular people make, sure, yeah, I guess you could say it's "a lot" of money. I mean it *is* a lot of money. But it's not enough money . . . for my, um, "lifestyle" . . . which means not enough money for my wife.

JO-ELLEN: You know what? Your wife sounds like a real bitch.

JERRY: Well, no. She isn't. I mean, it takes two to tango. On the other hand, some days, yeah. She is. She's not the most supportive person. And she expects, you know, me to deliver the goods. It's . . . you know, L.A. She needs her props.

JO-ELLEN: "Props"?

JERRY: Isn't that what you call it? Being a TV writer I'm supposed to be hip to all the lingo, but I'm not even sure what the term means. I think it means, jewelry and cars and facials and vacations in Hawaii and all that stuff.

JO-ELLEN: Wow. You get her all that?

JERRY: As much as I can.

(Jo-Ellen moves closer to Jerry.)

JO-ELLEN: What kind of car do you drive?

JERRY: A Mercedes. Laura has a Range Rover. We live in the Valley. We're a fucking cliché. Right car. Right spa. Right da-dee-dah-dah. But if you don't do it, then in my business, in my life, you stick out like a leper at the Mr. Universe contest.

JO-ELLEN: You make it sound terrible.

JERRY: Can I tell you something? I mean, we're never gonna see each other again. And I need to tell somebody, what's been happening to me, and maybe when I tell you, you'll understand . . . um, I'm sorry, you know, that I thought you were a hooker, but to be honest it was your smile that was so nice and warm and it touched me and I *needed* to be touched because I've been in a really bad place for the last six months, and it's been torture, what I've been going through. I'm in . . . I'm in love.

JO-ELLEN: With me?

JERRY: Oh, no. No. Did I just say that? I didn't mean to say that. No, I'm . . . in love with someone I was working with, an actress. And, you know, we went out for drinks and dinner to discuss the script and, anyway, we ended up . . . sleeping together and it was amazing, the most amazing thing ever. Nicole was so giving and loving and beautiful and she even thought I was great in bed. I'd never had passion like that. I thought about her day and night. We talked on the phone for hours and hours. Kept meeting at all these out-of-the-way Starbucks. I was planning to leave my wife, my kids. And then, I dunno what happened.

JO-ELLEN: Then?

JERRY: Then she got tired of me, I guess. She said she was "over" me. And I couldn't . . . let go. I went a little nuts,

I'd call her up just to listen to her voice on her voicemail. I flew to New York just to stand outside her apartment building. Just to see her. She wouldn't talk to me anymore. Told me to leave her alone. And that's why I had to come out here to Florida to get away from her and clear my head. And in fact, I thought, when you smiled at me that, maybe, I dunno, maybe having sex with someone new would like wipe her out of my heart. You know? I'm sorry. I didn't mean to burden you with all that.

JO-ELLEN: No. It's, you know, nice. I'm glad you told me. I can't believe she didn't fall in love with you, too.

JERRY: Yeah?

JO-ELLEN: Well, you're kind of sweet. I just met you, but that's the impression I get . . . but so . . . anyway, that's too bad that you're in love. Plus married on top of it. *(Beat)* I've never really been in love.

JERRY: Well, it's not something I would recommend at the moment, given my experience. Marriage *or* being in love.

JO-ELLEN: I feel bad for you.

JERRY: That's OK. But thanks.

(Jerry looks miserable.)

JO-ELLEN: No, I mean. You don't have to thank me. Really.

(Jo-Ellen kisses Jerry.)

JERRY: Whoa.

JO-ELLEN: Yeah.

(They both reach out for their beers and drink.)

JERRY: This is so ridiculous.

JO-ELLEN: It is. *(Bubbly)* But it's nice, too. It's fun. I'm having fun. I know it's hard to believe, but things are kind of boring around here most of the time.

JERRY: Well, this is fun for me, too. Really. If I came back to this room alone tonight, who knows what I might have done?

JO-ELLEN: No. Don't say that!

JERRY: Well, you know.

JO-ELLEN: Actually I do know. I know all about it.

(Pregnant pause. They start kissing again.)

JERRY: This is so crazy.

JO-ELLEN: Yeah.

JERRY: Nice, crazy.

JO-ELLEN: Yeah.

JERRY: And just think, it's for free.

JO-ELLEN *(Shoves him, laughing)*: Asshole!

JERRY: Well, I'm just saying. Never mind. I am an asshole.

JO-ELLEN: No you're not.

JERRY: You don't know me well enough to say that.

JO-ELLEN: I can tell. And besides, maybe I'm an asshole, too. You don't know.

JERRY: Maybe you are.

JO-ELLEN: Maybe I really am a hooker and you know, this is all a complicated setup.

JERRY: Yeah. Right. *(Suddenly looks worried)*

JO-ELLEN: I'm joking! You're such a funny guy! Can't you take a joke?

JERRY: Not lately I guess.

(Jerry finishes his beer, tosses it into the trash and gets another. He moves close to Jo-Ellen.)

Could you. Uh, would you? Kiss me? One more time?

(They kiss. A long kiss.)

Wow.

(The phone rings.)

(Picking up) Yeah? Oh. OK. Yeah. Uh, be right down. *(To Jo-Ellen)* Cab's here.

JO-ELLEN: Oh. OK.

JERRY *(To phone)*: She'll be right down. *(Hangs up. To Jo-Ellen)* So.

JO-ELLEN: So.

JERRY: Unless you know, you want to stay?

JO-ELLEN: Only if you want me to.

JERRY: Well. But, uh, your brother . . .

JO-ELLEN: My brother . . . Right.

JERRY: And, uh, the cab's already here.

JO-ELLEN: Right.

JERRY: I mean . . .

JO-ELLEN: No, you're right. I should go.

JERRY: I'm sorry if this was, you know, weird . . .

JO-ELLEN: No. No.

JERRY: We did have a nice talk.

JO-ELLEN: We did.

JERRY: I mean, I'd be happy if you . . .

(The phone rings again. Jerry picks up.)

She's coming. *(To Jo-Ellen)* So . . . um, it's been very nice meeting you, Jo-Ellen.

JO-ELLEN: Likewise, Jerry.

(They go to the door. Big hug. No kiss.)

JERRY: You really helped me out. Tonight.

JO-ELLEN: Yeah. Me, too.

(Uncomfortable pause.)

JERRY: Well, bye.

JO-ELLEN: Bye.

(Jerry opens the door. Jo-Ellen leaves. Jerry comes into the room. He tosses out her empty beer, finishes his. Laughs to himself.)

JERRY: You are such a fuck-head, Jerry.

(He laughs again. Then he picks up the remote, flips on the TV, CNN. He sits on the couch, sad.
A knock at the door.)

Just a minute!

(Jerry gets up, goes to the door and opens it. Jo-Ellen is standing there.)

JO-ELLEN: I can stay, but I can't stay the whole night.

(Blackout.)

ACT TWO

Same room. Morning, the curtains are drawn.

    There is knocking at the door. Then nothing. The knocking, firm, repeats.

    Jerry emerges in boxer shorts. His voice is cheery.

JERRY: That's OK. I don't need the room made up!

    (The knocking continues.)

    (Fuzzy, to himself) Fuck me. *(To the door)* JUST A SEC!

    (Jerry exits into the bathroom, returns as he throws on a bathrobe, goes to the door, opens it.
    Chet, thirty, and Boner, twenty-five, are standing there. They are dressed in industrial uniforms.)

CHET: Hi.
JERRY: 'Morning.
CHET: May we come in?

JERRY: Uh, actually, no. Did the, uh, "do not disturb" sign fall off my door? I was uh . . . just getting up actually.

CHET: Only be a minute.

(Chet and Boner enter and close the door behind them.)

JERRY: Listen it's just one lamp, and I'm checking out today, so I don't really care.

(Boner locks the door. He puts a paper bag down on a table. Chet goes to the window and flings open the drapes.)

I mean it's daytime now, I'm not going to even use it.

(Chet picks up an empty beer can, brings it to his nose, sniffs it. Jerry gets annoyed.)

You know what? Maybe I should call the front desk and they can straighten this out.

(Jerry moves toward the phone. Chet gets in his way.)

CHET: Don't do that. You don't wanna do that.

JERRY: Actually I do. I do want to do that. And I want you to leave.

CHET: Is that what you want?

JERRY: Uh-huh.

CHET: Well, fuck you.

JERRY: What?

CHET: Fuck . . . you.

(Boner snickers.)

JERRY: OK, now what is this? Who are you?

CHET: No, no, wrong question. Who are *you*?

BONER *(Smiling)*: Who are *you*? That's the question all right.

CHET: I mean, are you an *asshole*? Is that who you are? Mister ASS-HOLE? *(To his friend)* Boner, is that who he is?

BONER: Smells like one.

JERRY: C'mon. You got the wrong room. Get outta here.

(Jerry heads for the door. Boner stops him.)

CHET *(Pushing him around)*: Oh, no. We got the right room, asshole. 1626. Exactly the right room. Where the *asshole* lives.

JERRY: OK. *(Sits on couch)* What? What do you want?

CHET: Wanted to meet you. "Jerry."

JERRY: Hey. *(Stands)*

CHET: Fuck you. Sit down.

(Jerry sits again.)

I know your type. Guys like you. Guys in hotel rooms. With their Gold American Express card. Throwin' their weight around. What are you, Jewish?

JERRY: Oh, please.

CHET: Jewish. Sure. From Los Angeles. *(To Boner)* Boner, gimme a beer.

(Boner reaches into his bag, finds a few beers, hands one to Chet. Chet pops his beer, drinks. Boner does the same.)

(To Jerry) Want one?

JERRY: No, I don't want one. It is ten o'clock in the morning. I want you out of my room.

CHET: I thought you liked people coming to visit you?

(Boner goes into the bathroom. After a moment, we hear the toilet flushing.)

JERRY: *No* . . . I actually like to order room service, have a shower, put on some clothes, then maybe, *maybe* if I want to meet someone, I go out to do it.

CHET: Really.

(Boner reenters, wiping his hands on a big thick bath towel.)

BONER: This is a nice room. Only places I ever stayed were like motor courts. This is much nicer. Actually two rooms, isn't it?

JERRY: They call it a "suite."

BONER: Sweet. *(Laughs)* Sweeeeeet. Sweeeeeeeet! Souueeeeeee! Squeals like a pig. *(Laughs maniacally)*

(Chet isn't laughing. Neither is Jerry. Boner pulls a bag of dope out of his jacket and begins to roll joints.)

CHET: You like to party, Jew-boy?

BONER: He's a party boy.

CHET: You a party boy?

BONER: Ladies' man.

CHET: Ladies' man?

BONER: Mac Daddy.

CHET: You a Mac Daddy there, Jew-boy?

JERRY: I hope you understand that what you're doing here in my room is breaking the law. I'm not sure exactly what law you're breaking, but I guarantee you it is illegal.

CHET: Hey. SHUT THE FUCK UP!

(Chet is glowering at Jerry. Jerry decides to be quiet.)

BONER: Does this place have a minibar? I bet it does. Minibar. Bits of food, cashews and chocolates. Paintings on the walls. Cable TV. Nicer than my place. See, you could *live* here. You could just move in and live here. And people do that. I've read about people who do stuff like that. Live in their hotel room. Never leave. Order room service 'round the clock. I think the Sex Pistols lived in a hotel room. *(He lights a joint, takes a drag. To Jerry)* Want some?

(Jerry doesn't answer.)

Suit yourself. *(He takes another hit)* "Skunkweed," it stinks to high heaven, but it will get you fucked up good.

(Boner chuckles and passes the joint to Chet. Chet takes a big hit, keeping an eye on Jerry. He lets the smoke out in a long stream into Jerry's face. Jerry doesn't look at him.)

CHET *(To Jerry)*: Fuck you. Fuck you. Fuck you. Fuck you. Fuck you. Fuck you.

(A cell phone rings. It's Chet's. Chet finds the phone in his jacket and answers it.)

Hey. *(Beat)* Yeah. *(He hangs up)*

JERRY: What was that? The "signal"? Ooooh. Now what happens? I'm breathless with anticipation! *(Beat)* You know what? You guys are like a bad movie.

CHET: Hey, friend, I'd be quiet if I were you. Because in my back pocket is a buck knife. The one I use for gutting deer. It's nice and shiny, oiled and sharp. But I'll tell you a secret. I don't mind getting it wet. At all.

(Long beat, letting that sink in.
Chet passes the joint back to Boner.)

BONER *(Off a hit)*: You know what you call this, Chet? The lap of luxury. Lap O' Luxury. Like *Lap Dance* of Luxury. Like *lapping up* the luxury. Licking it. Sucking on it like a big giant tit.

(Looking around, through the doors, etc.) King-size bed. Widescreen plasma TV. Big, thick towels. Air-conditioning. A magnificent view. This is the way the other half lives, man. This is what you call "the good life." Just turn on the

SKUNKWEED

Pay-Per-View and order up room service and get wasted. The good life. The fucking good life. What everybody wants and nobody gets.

CHET: Oh, somebody gets it all right. Jerry gets it.

BONER: True.

CHET: Good ol' Jerry.

BONER: Good ol' Jerry.

(Chet picks up the phone, preparing to call room service.)

Room-fucking-service. Steaks and chops. A basket of freshly baked breads with pats of creamery butter on the side. A mixed salad with flower petals sprinkled on top. Berry pie and chocolate cake iced with chocolate frosting. Heinekens, Perriers and a jug of hot coffee brewed from freshly ground, freshly roasted, Jamaican coffee beans. A tiny itsy-bitsy pitcher of cream nestled in a bed of ice. A pink carnation in a stem vase.

CHET *(He calls; into the phone)*: Yeah, hello, I want to order some room service? [. . .] That's right, 1626. Mr. Goldberg. [. . .] Uh-huh. Ummm. You got eggs? [. . .] No, none a that fancy shit, just fried eggs, sunny-side up. Six orders. [. . .] Yeah, that's right. [. . .] Huh? All of it. Bacon and sausage *and* ham. [. . .] That's right. Six. No make it seven. And ummm. Pie, what kind of pie you got? [. . .] Yeah? OK. A slice of each one of those. And ummm, two big jugs of coffee. [. . .] What? [. . .] Sure, croissants, good, bunch of those. And doughnuts, you got any doughnuts? [. . .] Cool. [. . .] Orange juice, yeah, yeah. All that. All that. You think of anything else, you just stick it on there, OK, darlin'? [. . .] You, too, bye.

(Chet hangs up.)

JERRY: And when the food arrives, you think I'm just gonna sit here and not say anything?

CHET: That's why they call it a suite, asshole, 'cause it has two rooms.

JERRY: Who the fuck are you?

CHET: Oh, you *know* who I am.

JERRY: I don't.

CHET: Take a big fucking guess, smart guy.

(There is a knock on the door.)

BONER: Shit, that was fast!

(Chet shoots a look at Boner and goes to the door. He peeks through the peephole and opens it. Jo-Ellen and two other women, Christine, thirty-five, and Rainbow, twenty, enter. Christine has a small baby in her arms.)

CHRISTINE: Hey, honey.

(Chet busses Christine as she passes him into the room.)

CHET *(To Jerry)*: Figured it out yet, asswipe?

JO-ELLEN *(To Jerry, as she enters)*: He made me tell him where I was last night.

CHET: Jerry, this is Christine . . .

CHRISTINE: Hi.

CHET: What'd you bring the baby for?

CHRISTINE: Who am I supposed to leave her with, Chet? Jo-Ellen? Duh?

CHET: And this is Rainbow.

RAINBOW: Hi.

CHET: And, of course, you know my *sister*, Jo-Ellen.

JO-ELLEN *(To Jerry)*: See, I always get home by midnight, so he, you know, he *knew*. And I thought if I said, you know, I met a nice guy from Los Angeles, then that would be better. But it wasn't. I'm sorry.

JERRY: It's OK. I mean, not really. But it's not your fault. It's OK.

SKUNKWEED

CHET: No, it's not. It's not "OK." See? It's not "OK."

(Rainbow goes over to Boner and they kiss. Christine exits into the bedroom with her baby.)

BONER: Hey, baby.

RAINBOW: This is so weird, Boner.

BONER: No, it's not. It's cool.

RAINBOW: Well, it's kinda cool but it's also weird. At the same time. Cool and weird.

(Christine returns.)

CHRISTINE: The baby's sleeping, so everybody should be a little quiet. And that means *you*, Chet. *(Settling herself, as if she's visiting a neighbor. To Jerry)* Jo-Ellen says you write TV shows?

JERRY: Uh-huh.

CHRISTINE: Which ones?

JERRY: Ever hear of *High Incident*?

CHRISTINE: No. Sorry.

JERRY: Yeah, well, it was a few years ago. But I dunno: *Lost, Law & Order* . . .

CHRISTINE: Have you ever met Will Smith?

CHET: Jesus, Christine, of all the people to ask him about, you have to ask him about some nigger.

CHRISTINE: Chet, do *not* use that language around me, I swear, I will take Danielle and I will walk right out of here, right now.

CHET: I'm just saying . . .

CHRISTINE: Never mind what you're saying. I know what you're saying, 'cause you always say the same damn thing. It is beyond me how anyone who calls himself a born-again Christian can have the attitudes that you have toward Negro people. And the Spanish. And pretty much everybody. You are a negative man, Chet, and it is disturbing to me that the father of my child is so prejudiced and narrow-minded. And I'm not even getting into the endless cussing you do.

(Silence.)

JERRY: I met him once at a party. For two minutes. Will Smith. I mean.

CHRISTINE: You *did?*

JERRY: Yeah. Nice guy, actually. Everyone who works with him says so. Smart.

RAINBOW: Oh, that is *so* cool. Will Smith!

CHRISTINE: Who else have you met, Jerry?

CHET: Never mind who he met! He met my sister, OK? In the *Biblical* sense of the word, he met my sister.

(Chet glowers at Christine, she ignores him and turns to Boner.)

CHRISTINE: Are those beers, Boner? May I have one please?

(Boner hands her a beer. She takes it with dainty finesse.)

RAINBOW: What about me?

(Boner hands Rainbow a beer.)

Thank you.

BONER: You want one Jo-Ellen?

CHET: She's had enough, just keep your beer to yourself.

(Rainbow clicks on the TV set with the remote control. She's instantly transfixed.)

JO-ELLEN: Chet.

CHET: What?

JO-ELLEN: What are you going to do?

CHET: I'm going to enjoy some Jewish hospitality.

JERRY: Can I put on some clothes please?

CHET: Oh, he was so ready to take them off, now he wants to put 'em back on. Nothing makes this guy happy.

(Jerry stands up and gets in Chet's face.)

JERRY: Hey, you know what? Fuck you! I didn't do anything. Your sister's an adult, she wants to come up here and . . . have a good time with me . . . that's *her* choice. What's it got to do with you? Huh? I could have you arrested. I could have you put in jail for what you're doing right now. You're holding me against my will. Kidnapping me. Now, I'm going to go into that bedroom and I'm going to get my clothes and put them on and leave, because I have a plane to catch. *(Stands)*

CHET: Hey. I don't remember anyone saying you could get up. Asshole.

(Chet pushes Jerry back into the chair.)

JO-ELLEN: Chet!

(Chet gets himself another beer.)

CHET: I'm not here to debate you, Mr. Los Angeles. And I don't have to explain myself neither. I'm just here. OK? That's all you gotta know. Like a fucking headache. So you just sit there and shut the fuck up.

(In a fit of anger, he smashes his beer into the wall, spraying foam all over the place.)

FUCK!

(Chet sucks on the gap between his thumb and forefinger. He's hurt his hand, it hurts a lot. He exits into the bathroom.)

JO-ELLEN: I didn't know you knew Will Smith.

JERRY: You didn't ask.

(Beat.)

CHRISTINE: Chet is very immature. But you know what? You shouldna had sex with his dead mama's baby daughter!

RAINBOW *(Still watching TV)*: Dr. Phil, my favorite!

CHRISTINE: Oh, today he's doing a special on mothers who lose their temper a lot. *(To bathroom)* CHET! MAYBE YOU SHOULD WATCH IT.

(Sounds of things breaking and crashing in the bathroom.)

JO-ELLEN: I'm so sorry, Jerry.

JERRY: Don't be. Up until about twenty minutes ago, I was a very happy man.

JO-ELLEN: Me, too.

JERRY *(Quietly, to Jo-Ellen)*: You made me feel very good last night. You made me feel taken care of. You made me feel . . . good . . . in a deep way. You touched something in me that had not been touched in a long time . . .

(Chet comes roaring out of the bathroom.)

CHET: SO HELP ME GOD IF YOU DO NOT SHUT THE FUCK UP I AM GOING TO CUT THAT EVERLO-VING TONGUE OUT OF YOUR SEMITIC SKULL. NOW SHUT UP! SHUT UP! SHUT UP! *(To Jo-Ellen)* And *you*. You don't wanna make things any worse than they already are.

(Everybody goes quiet. Only the TV can be heard. Then:)

BONER: I saw this Discovery Channel program about how the Mayans would make a cord out of thorns and pull it through a guy's tongue as a kind of sacrifice. They did a lot of shit like that. That's something you don't see too much these days. People getting their tongues cut out. Used to do it all the time in the old days. In all those Indian movies. And then there was that *Twilight Zone* about the guy who couldn't stop talking and he made a bet he could shut up for a year and then he won the bet, but it turned out he'd cut his tongue off?

(More silence.)

RAINBOW: That's like that guy who got a hair wrapped around his eyeball? It's like the hair got in his eye, and then it went around and around and he almost lost his eye!

BONER: Or like the guy who got his balls caught in the belt sander? Tore 'em right off. Went to the doctor's office with his balls in a paper sack.

RAINBOW: Wow. That's true?

BONER: Sure it's true, read it in the newspaper.

(There is a knock on the door.)

VOICE *(Off)*: Room service.

CHET: Boner.

(Boner gets up, takes Jerry by the arm, and gently begins leading him into the bedroom.)

BONER: I also have a knife in my back pocket. Just so you know.

CHET: Hey, Jerry. Don't let Boner fool ya. He's all heart. Served five years for attempted manslaughter. Almost killed a Hell's Angel with a pool cue. He's a sweet guy, but you don't wanna get him angry.

(Boner walks Jerry into the bedroom and closes the door.)

CHRISTINE: You ordered food, Chet?

CHET: Oh yeah.

RAINBOW: Yay, food!

(Chet opens the front door and two Waiters wheel in two rolling carts heaped with food.)

WAITER *(Cheery)*: And how is everybody this morning?

CHET: Great. Everybody's great. Having a wonderful time. Just roll it over there, *(Reading the Waiter's name tag)* "Bruce." Rainbow, let the guy get in there.

(The Waiters position the food, uncover the hot dishes, etc.)

WAITER *(Handing Chet the check)*: Here you go, Mr. Goldberg, the service is included but if you wish to add a tip, it would be greatly appreciated.

CHET *(Loud enough for Jerry to hear)*: Of course I'm gonna leave a tip. You think just 'cause I'm Jewish I'm not gonna leave a tip? *(Confidential, to the Waiter)* See that's the problem with the world these days. Too much prejudice. Just because my people killed the Lord Jesus Christ, doesn't mean we're cheap. There you go.

WAITER *(Reading the bill)*: Oh, thank you. Very generous. Would you like me to pour out your coffee, Mr. Goldberg?

CHET: Nah, that's OK. But, hey, Bruce, you got any cigars down there in the gift shop?

WAITER: We do.

CHET: What do you have that's good?

WAITER: Macanudos?

CHET: Great. Send me up a box. Put it on the tab.

WAITER: With pleasure, Mr. Goldberg. Now you folks have a nice breakfast.

(The two Waiters leave.)

CHET: You hungry, Christine, 'cause I'm not gonna eat all of this myself.

CHRISTINE: I shouldn't.

(Christine picks up a croissant.)

Oh I love these.

CHET: Good.

CHRISTINE: Mmmmmmm. Chet, I think you're going a little too far.

CHET: Oh, you think so, huh? Too far, huh? I know who went too far.

RAINBOW: Who?

CHRISTINE: I think you've made your point.

CHET: Just eat.

RAINBOW: Where'd Boner go?

CHRISTINE: He's in the bedroom with Jerry.

RAINBOW: Why?

CHET: Boner! Get back in here!

(Boner comes back in with Jerry. Jerry's wearing pants under his robe. Boner grabs a doughnut, munches contendedly.)

JERRY: Look, I've been thinking about this. I think you have a misunderstanding about me.

CHET: Oh, you do?

JERRY: Yes. I think you think I'm some kind of big shot or something. Some kind of show-biz asshole. But that's just not true.

CHET: First of all, Mr. Goldberg, don't tell me what I think. Second of all, I don't have a misunderstanding about anything. You have a misunderstanding about us, buddy. You think you can come down here to our home, to where we live and comingle with the locals and get away with it. Hey, I got news for ya, this isn't Thailand, pal. This is America. And you want to play, you have to pay.

BONER: Hey, Chet, did I ever tell you about my idea for a movie? Because I was telling Jerry in the bedroom and he thinks it's not such a bad idea. He thinks he can make a few phone calls and set it up.

RAINBOW: Oh, Boner, that would be so great!

CHET: Make a few phone calls, huh?

BONER: Yeah. Call his contacts.

CHET: How's he gonna do that with two broken arms?

JO-ELLEN: CHET! Stop it!

CHET: You be quiet. Eat some eggs or something. Boner, eat some eggs. Rainbow. Everybody eat eggs.

BONER: I'm allergic to eggs.

CHET: Well, eat 'em anyway. You, Jerry. You hungry?

(Jerry doesn't answer.)

CHRISTINE: Chet, um, don't you have to go to work today?

CHET: I took a sick day.

CHRISTINE: Oh, you did? I thought you'd already taken all your sick days this year.

CHET: Let me worry about that.

CHRISTINE *(Sarcastic)*: Oh, OK. *(To Boner)* What about you, Boner? Are you losing money today, too?

BONER: Nah, I got laid off last month. I don't have to go in to pick up my unemployment check until tomorrow.

(Chet goes to the minibar and takes out a bunch of bottles. He starts uncapping them and drinking.)

CHET: What kind of faggot would drink whiskey out a little tiny bottle like this?

RAINBOW: Hey, Jerry, did you ever meet Madonna?

JERRY: As a matter of fact, yes.

(Chet drinks four of the bottles and tosses them through the bathroom door into the bathtub. We can hear the glass breaking.)

SKUNKWEED

RAINBOW: What was she like?

(The baby starts to cry in the next room. Christine goes in to see her.)

JERRY: You know, it happened so fast, I don't really remember.

RAINBOW: Was she pretty?

JERRY: Oh sure. I mean, she's Madonna, right?

RAINBOW: Wow. I can't even imagine your life. Flying around, meeting famous people. Staying in a room like this.

JERRY: This room isn't so great.

RAINBOW: It isn't?

JERRY: Well, it's not Shutters. It's not the Four Seasons. It's a Westin for God's sake.

RAINBOW: Westin's good, isn't it?

(Chet drinks more of the booze.)

CHET: Eecchh. What is this shit?

(The baby has stopped crying. Christine reappears in the door.)

CHRISTINE: OK, Chet, this is getting really boring. Why don't we make a game plan here.

CHET: No game plan.

CHRISTINE: Chet, I don't know about you, but I have food shopping to do, there's a wash in the machine and Little Chet gets dropped off at three.

CHET *(Sullen)*: I don't know what I want to do. My brain is like a vacuum. I'm so fucking angry. I'm doing everything I can just to keep myself from killing this fucker.

CHRISTINE: Well, that's not very constructive, is it?

CHET: Christine . . .

CHRISTINE: It reminds me when we were at Sonny's Diner last week for dinner? And you couldn't decide whether you wanted the baby back ribs or the three-for-one special. And what happened?

CHET: Never mind about that.

CHRISTINE: No, answer me, Chet. What happened? I'll tell you what happened. You couldn't make up your mind. So *then* what happened?

CHET: Christine.

CHRISTINE: You got angry at *me*. And then what happened?

CHET: Stop it!

CHRISTINE: We left. We didn't have dinner at Sonny's, did we, Chet? Because you didn't know what you wanted. And so you didn't do anything. And you know what, Chet? Not doing anything is the same as making a decision. It's being a *victim*.

CHET: This has nothing to do with that. This has to do with a very fucked-up situation. A situation where some big shot thinks he can just roll over me, roll over my family. Do whatever he wants. Take whatever he wants. The same old story, my whole life, people just doing whatever they want, and I'm supposed shut up and take it. Well, I'm not gonna do that. Not this time. There's gonna be payback. OK? There's gonna be pain.

(Chet goes back to the minibar and drinks.)

CHRISTINE: It still comes down to, whatchoo gonna do?

BONER: Normally, if this were like a movie, we'd get money off of him. Like that.

JERRY: You want money? Is that what this is about? There's my wallet on top of the TV. I have about a hundred and twenty bucks in there. Knock yourself out.

(Boner grabs the wallet. He starts taking things out of it, putting them on the coffee table.)

RAINBOW *(Picking up photos)*: Oh, are these your kids? Cute!

CHRISTINE: You have kids?

JERRY: Two. Boy and a girl. I'm gonna miss my flight.

CHRISTINE: Same as us! How old are they?

JERRY: Uh. Girl's two, boy's six. I think. Yeah. Six.

RAINBOW: Aren't they sweet, Christine? Look Jo-Ellen!

JO-ELLEN *(Taking a cursory glance at the photos)*: Yeah. Sweet. *(She moves off to a corner by herself)*

BONER: Credit cards.

CHET: Boner, what the fuck are we gonna do with credit cards? What are you, an asshole? We're gonna take a credit card down to the Best Buy and what, charge up a bunch of TV sets, get arrested out in the parking lot?

BONER: We could sell the cards. I know guys who'd buy 'em.

CHET: No.

CHRISTINE: So, you all live in L.A.?

JERRY: Yeah. It's nice. We have a swimming pool. We have a lawn. Trees. It's really really nice.

RAINBOW: Sounds so beautiful!

CHET: Look. Look. Here's the deal. Asshole. You did a bad thing. Do you know you did a bad thing?

JERRY: No.

CHET: Well, I'll tell you this, we're not goin' anywhere until you at least admit that you're an asshole.

JERRY: No.

CHET: FUCK IT, YOU PIECE OF SHIT! FUCK YOU!

JERRY: No. Fuck you!

CHET: OK. OK. Well, whether you admit it or not. You have to pay the penalty. There a bank card in there, Boner?

BONER: Uh . . . yup.

CHET: What's the PIN number?

JERRY: Oh, come on!

CHET: Card like this, I bet there's money in there. Max it to the limit, I bet I can squeeze out a grand. How's that sound? A thousand bucks—penalty for being an asshole.

JERRY: This is so fucked-up.

CHET: Oh really? You're just figuring that out? Hey, Boner, lemme see that license?

(Boner hands over the license. Chet scans it.)

Name. Address. Won't be that hard to give your little lady a call.

JERRY: OK. Look. Sure. A thousand bucks. That's the most you can get out of it, unless my wife already hit it today, but she's on the West Coast so, probably not.

CHET: PIN?

JERRY: 1-1-7-7.

BONER: Lucky.

CHET: 1-1-7-7. OK. I'll be right back. C'mon, Christine.

CHRISTINE: The baby has to be fed.

CHET: Well, Boner has to stay here, he can't come. And I'm not goin' by myself. Jo-Ellen, c'mon, you started this.

(Jo-Ellen gets her things.)

Just . . . you know, everybody chill out. We'll be back in ten minutes. *(Chet grabs Jerry's wallet and his credit cards, etc.)* I'll just take this as insurance.

(Chet and Jo-Ellen leave. Boner picks at the food.)

CHRISTINE: He is so irritating some times.

JERRY: Irritating. Yeah, that's one word for it.

(Rainbow fiddles with the stereo system, puts on a hip-hop station. Boner's pretty wasted and relaxing with the food.)

RAINBOW: You know what? Everybody's just got to relax around here.

(Rainbow starts moving to the beat.)

CHRISTINE: Rainbow! The baby!

RAINBOW: The baby's OK. C'mon Chrissie, dance with me.

(Christine dances reluctantly. Boner leans back and checks out the two girls.)

BONER: Now this is living. *(Winks at Jerry)* Beautiful girls. Fine food. Wall-to-wall carpeting. This is the life of the movie stars.

JERRY *(Watching the girls)*: More or less.

(Rainbow pulls at Boner.)

RAINBOW: Dance with us!
BONER: Oh, no. Wrong guy.

(Rainbow goes after Jerry.)

RAINBOW: C'mon, Jerry!

(Jerry won't budge.)

JERRY: That's all right. I'll pass.
RAINBOW: Boner, tell Jerry to dance with us.
BONER: Jerry . . .
JERRY: Oh, Jesus!
BONER: What do you know about Jesus?!
RAINBOW: Please?

(Rainbow tugs Jerry to his feet. Christine is delighted.
Rainbow and Christine dance on either side of Jerry, laughing. The absurdity of the situation makes him laugh. He dances. He gets into it. Boner watches with stoned, lidded eyes.
Things go a little nuts with Jerry spinning around, holding on to each of the girls. Finally the song ends. Christine peeks in on the baby. Jerry collapses breathless, Rainbow smiles at him.)

CHRISTINE *(Regarding the baby)*: She's sleeping . . . like a baby!
Oh, Rainbow, you have your bag with you?
RAINBOW: Uh-huh.
CHRISTINE: Do you have your phone?
RAINBOW: I do!
CHRISTINE: You thinking what I'm thinking?
RAINBOW: Oh yeah! Let's call somebody.
CHRISTINE: No!
RAINBOW: What?
CHRISTINE: Take a picture. With Jerry!
RAINBOW: Oh, yeah. Chrissie, that's such a good idea!
CHRISTINE *(To Jerry)*: Will you?
JERRY: What?
CHRISTINE: Take a picture with us?
JERRY: Why?
RAINBOW: You're like the most *famous* person we've *ever* met.
JERRY: I'm not famous.
RAINBOW: More famous than we are. A lot more famous.
CHRISTINE: Boner. Stop eating. Take our picture.

(Rainbow hands Boner the picture phone.)

BONER: OK. It's pretty small. How do I do this?

(Rainbow shows him. Then jumps onto the couch with Jerry and Christine.)

RAINBOW: Just do this, here, see?
CHRISTINE *(Tickling Jerry)*: Hey there, Mr. Grumpy Face.

(She makes him smile.)

BONER: OK. OK. Everybody say "Cheez Whiz."
JERRY, RAINBOW AND CHRISTINE: "CHEEZ-WHIZ."

(Jerry and the women laugh. They start snuggling into him.)

CHRISTINE: See, that isn't so hard. *(Glancing at his crotch)* Or is it?

RAINBOW: Hey, I can see why Jo-Ellen likes you.

CHRISTINE: Oh, he's cute all right. She said he has muscles, too.

RAINBOW: You can't tell with his clothes on. Do you have muscles, Jerry?

JERRY: Uh, sure. I work out. You know. Treadmill. Push-ups. Dumbbells. I work out just enough to get minor pecs, biceps, you know.

RAINBOW: I like a skinny guy.

BONER: Hey!

RAINBOW: Boner has got himself a little pot belly now.

BONER: Hey, how 'bout this? I kick this guy's ass right now in front of you two and you can figure who has the bigger muscles?

RAINBOW: He'd probably kick *your* ass, Boner. He's from L.A. People in L.A. take, like, martial arts and stuff like that.

BONER: Yeah, well I got a little martial arts training myself. Amazing the shit you learn when you're stuck in a cage with a bunch of crazy killers.

RAINBOW: Well, you know what? Sometimes a guy is sexy, without needing to swear and fight and drink and all that stupid stuff. Sometimes a guy is just cute. *(She snuggles Jerry)*

BONER: And sometimes a guy gets a new asshole cut into his face.

RAINBOW: And sometimes a girl likes to have some civilized attention for a change.

BONER: What are you talking about, "civilized attention"? You trying to piss me off, Rain?

RAINBOW: Just because I have your name tattooed on my ass, doesn't mean you own me, big guy.

BONER: Hey, OK. Uh . . . I don't know what's gotten into you. But I recommend you stop. Right now. 'Cause you're getting me very, very angry. *(Furrows his brow)* Fuck! All those eggs. My stomach is killing me. *(Scrutinizes Jerry)* If I went into the bathroom, you wouldn't try anything, would ya?

JERRY: I don't have a quarrel with you . . . um . . . Boner. And besides, I really do like your screenplay idea.

BONER: You do?

JERRY: I said I did. It's got a great arc.

BONER: Wow. *(Clutches his stomach)* OK. Well. Everybody just stay doing what you're doing, and I'll be back in about . . . whatever.

(Boner snatches up a magazine and heads into the bathroom. He slams the door.)

(From behind the door) BROKEN GLASS ALL OVER THE PLACE IN HERE! ALMOST CUT MY ASS! FUCK!

(Jerry, Christine and Rainbow sit. Christine picks up a doughnut and eats it with dainty precision. Rainbow continues to flirt with him.)

CHRISTINE: Your kids are cute.

JERRY: Thanks.

CHRISTINE: So there's something I don't understand.

JERRY: Uh-huh.

CHRISTINE: You're married, right?

JERRY: Uh-huh.

CHRISTINE: For how long?

JERRY: Eleven years in June.

RAINBOW: Oh, that's the same as us! You have the nicest brown eyes.

JERRY: Thanks.

CHRISTINE: But Jo-Ellen told us that you and your wife aren't getting along.

JERRY: That's the general idea.

CHRISTINE: You told Jo-Ellen you thought she was a prostitute?

RAINBOW: But that you've never been with a prostitute?

JERRY: Jo-Ellen has really been filling you in.

RAINBOW: Have you ever been with a prostitute, Jerry?

JERRY: No!

CHRISTINE: How about a call girl?

JERRY: "Call girl"?

CHRISTINE: "Escort," whatever. Isn't that what you all call it out in L.A.?

JERRY: Listen, I'm not that kind of guy, OK?

CHRISTINE: You never did nothing sneaky, behind your wife's back?

RAINBOW: All those sexy women in L.A.?

JERRY: Many sexy women.

RAINBOW: You did something.

CHRISTINE: What'd you do, Jerry. Tell us. Before Boner comes back.

RAINBOW: It's OK, Jerry. We're your friends.

CHRISTINE: An actress I bet.

JERRY: This is the most absurd situation I have ever . . .

CHRISTINE: What happened?

JERRY: I don't want to tell you about my life.

CHRISTINE: You had a love affair with an actress? You did, didn't you?

JERRY: You say that like you know what you're talking about.

CHRISTINE: I know men.

RAINBOW: Madonna?

JERRY: No! *(Beat)* Look, she was in a pilot I worked on. She was from New York. I was show runner. I cast her. We shot the pilot, I fell in love with her. She was so beautiful. So loving. The pilot never got picked up. No series. She had to go back to New York. Things cooled off. End of story. Broken heart.

CHRISTINE: You're saying that she fell out of love with you because her pilot didn't get picked up?

JERRY: Uh . . . maybe.

RAINBOW: Did your wife find out?

JERRY: She suspected. So that's why things have been a little rocky. But see, it's her fault in the first place that I needed the attention that, you know, Nicole, gave me. Laura just wasn't meeting my needs. She wasn't there for me.

CHRISTINE: OK. So . . . you're married. You had an affair and your heart is broken. So, ummm, why did you sleep with Jo-Ellen?

JERRY: Jo-Ellen's very sweet. Very loving. I guess it felt right.

CHRISTINE: Yeah, but, you can't just go around doing things just because they feel right.

JERRY: Your husband has impressed that fact on me.

CHRISTINE: No. I mean. Chet's kind of overreacting, but still, don't you *know* what you want to do? Who you want to be with? I mean, excuse my French, but shit or get off the pot. What about the kids?

JERRY: That's what everybody says. "What about the kids?" What *about* the kids? Fuck the kids! What about me? What about *my* happiness?

CHRISTINE: Yeah, but you know, you're married. You gotta figure that out.

JERRY: Look. We went to couples therapy. I did chores, I made the bed. I "listened" to her.

CHRISTINE: Yeah, but see . . . You're right about Jo-Ellen being a grown-up and all that. She is. We all are. But the thing is, she . . .

RAINBOW: Christine!

CHRISTINE: She . . . I shouldn't be telling you this . . . but . . . she kinda fell for you.

JERRY: Well, I like her, too. A lot.

CHRISTINE: No. See that's not what I'm saying. It's not about the sex part or if everybody's playing by the rules or any of that. It's about the part where you were *nice* to her. And from what she tells me, she was nice to you. And that's, you know, that's being intimate. Which, I know your wife's not here right now, but isn't that what you should be doing with *her*?

JERRY: My wife is a cold bitch.

CHRISTINE: Well, it's no wonder! Her husband is sticking his noodle into every girl who says hel-lo.

RAINBOW: Christine!

JERRY: Hey, you don't know, all right?

CHRISTINE: You met my husband, of course I know. I know all about difficult people. But see, I *love* him. I love *all* of him. The good stuff and the difficult. That's . . . marriage.

(Jerry gets up and walks away.)

JERRY: Whatever. I guess. I dunno.

CHRISTINE: "For better or for worse." You promised. The better part's easy. It's the worse that's tough.

JERRY: But—

CHRISTINE: You do know what I'm talking about. I *know* you know.

JERRY: Yeah.

RAINBOW: This is like *so* much better than *Dr. Phil*!

(Boner emerges from the bathroom.)

BONER: Everybody still here. Good.

(Boner goes to the food, picks up something, takes a bite and throws it down in disgust.)

Fuck me. It's eleven A.M. and I am *wasted*.

CHRISTINE: It's your own damn fault.

(Christine exits to the bedroom to check on the baby.)

RAINBOW: You wanna lie down, baby?

(Jerry picks up the photos of his kids and looks at them.)

BONER: I can't. Chet comes back, finds me asleep, I'm fucked. You got anything in your bag there? Some white cross or crystal maybe?

RAINBOW: Why would I have crystal meth in my bag, Boner!

BONER: 'Cause you're a freak?

RAINBOW: Well, that's true. But actually I did all the crank last weekend when I was cleaning the house.

BONER: And you didn't give me any?

(Boner gets himself another beer.)

RAINBOW: You didn't *ask*. I mean, Boner, I was like washing the kitchen ceilings. I was vacuuming the *dog*. You don't have to be a rocket scientist to figure out I was speeding my cheeks off.

BONER: Hey, Jerry. You know, since my idea has such a good story arc, we could give it to a star now, before even the screenplay is written. Wouldn't it be easier to set it up at a studio with a star attached?

JERRY: How did you learn about all that?

BONER: Like, Will Smith, I mean the story's kind of not for a black guy, but Will Smith, he can do just about anything. And Madonna's always looking for a project, right?

JERRY: Stop. Boner. You're scaring me.

BONER: I mean, I don't even need to write it. I'll just take "story by" credit. *You* can write it. Or you could be an executive producer and we could go to someone on the A-list, not that I'm saying you're not A-list, Jerry, but you know what I mean.

(Christine reenters with the baby in her arms. She watches Jerry with a steady gaze, which he avoids.)

JERRY: Yeah. I do. I know exactly what you mean, Boner.

RAINBOW: You know, this is so cool that you and Boner are gonna to be working together, Jerry. Because my secret dream, my whole life, has been to go to Hollywood and be part of all that. It would just like be the ultimate. Because you know, our life is nice. It is. But it's so normal. You people,

SKUNKWEED

you folks who get to really be part of the fantasy, I mean, let's face it, you're living the *dream*. You're livin' *my* dream. And I know it requires a lot of work and a lot of luck, but I'm ready to work, and miracles *do* happen. And I know if I *believe*, if I really really believe, *anything* is possible.

BONER: I feel the same way.

RAINBOW: And, you know, Boner called me a freak before, but I'm really not. It's not like I'm sniffing drugs every day. I know people like that, speed freaks, complete waste-oids, and I'm definitely *not* one of them. So I don't want you to think that about me, Jerry. I'm ready to make my dreams come true just like you did. That's why it's been so inspiring to meet you. You're a powerful example.

JERRY: You don't know me. You don't know anything about my life.

RAINBOW: Jerry, it's like we've always known you!

JERRY: No.

RAINBOW: We know you and we love you.

JERRY: No. No. I object. You've come in here, and you've held me hostage and you've humiliated me and you've told me off, but there's one thing I will not concede and that is that you have any insight whatsoever to my life.

RAINBOW: Oh, Jerry. I thought we were friends!

JERRY: No. We are *not* friends. We are not anything. I'm just passing through.

RAINBOW: Christine, say something!

CHRISTINE: I agree with Jerry. Completely.

JERRY: Thank you for that crumb of sanity.

BONER: Well, I sure as hell don't! We got something going here. We bonded with each other, Jerry. You and me. I can understand why you might be a little pissed off, but we'll pay you back for the eggs and doughnuts.

RAINBOW: Yeah, we'll pay you back. Don't be mad.

BONER: No reason to be mad.

RAINBOW: *Please* don't be mad. *(Flirty)* Plus you're really a good dancer.

JERRY: Look, I'm not the one who's angry. I'm not the one who busts into a stranger's hotel room and threatens them. OK? I'm not the one who lectures other people about their sex lives. I didn't start all this shit.

CHRISTINE: Of course you did!

JERRY: Did not!

CHRISTINE: Did!

JERRY: Didn't!

CHRISTINE: You did!

JERRY: You have some nerve, lady. Wasn't it your big buddy Jesus who said, "Let he who is without sin cast the first stone"?

RAINBOW: How did you know that?

JERRY: I took a course in college.

CHRISTINE: I didn't throw any stones at you. I was trying to be helpful.

JERRY: I don't need your help. I don't need any of you.

RAINBOW: Jerry!

CHRISTINE: I saw a drowning man and I threw him a lifeline.

JERRY: Keep your lifeline.

CHRISTINE: I'm sorry. But I see someone as unhappy as you are and I just can't help myself.

JERRY: Who says I'm unhappy?

CHRISTINE: That's what you told Jo-Ellen.

JERRY: What did she do, replay every word of what happened last night?

CHRISTINE: No.

RAINBOW: She did say you're a very imaginative lover.

JERRY: Oh, fuck me!

CHRISTINE: I'm sorry, Jerry, if I overstepped.

RAINBOW: Me, too.

BONER: Yeah, and I'm really, really sorry.

(Everyone's kind of down, eyes on Jerry, as the door bursts open.)

CHET: OK. Everybody. Time to roll.

(Chet throws Jerry's wallet and room key card on the coffee table.)

(Sensing the mood in the room) What's going on here? Why all the long faces? Boner, did he try something?

BONER: No. Uh. We were just telling Jerry how sorry we were. You know, to have bothered him.

CHET: What?!

RAINBOW: Maybe you should say you're sorry, too, Chet.

CHET: I'm not saying shit. What's wrong with you people?

JERRY: So did you take the thousand?

CHRISTINE: Where's Jo-Ellen, Chet?

CHET: In the car. She didn't want to come up.

JERRY: You took the thousand?

CHET: You know, I saw what was in that account. If I camped out here for a few days, we could do real well by you.

JERRY: But you took a thousand? I just need to know for my accountant.

CHET: I coulda taken five.

JERRY: But . . .

CHET: C'mon, Christine, hurry it up.

JERRY: Are you finished meting out the pain?

CHET: Listen, pal, you gotta problem? I'm tellin' ya we're leaving, and you got your wallet back, and that's that.

JERRY: You're really leaving? No big surprises? Something bad, when I least expect it?

CHET: Something bad already happened, OK? You were born. But that's not for me to rectify. It's up to Somebody a lot more important than me, the Big Guy Upstairs. So . . . so that's it. We're gone. And you can go back to your happy-go-lucky life. Christine, get Danielle. Boner, let's go.

RAINBOW: Jerry, even if you don't think we're friends, I'll always think of you as my friend. And I hope you have a lot of success with your TV pilot.

JERRY: Thank you.

RAINBOW: What's it called?

JERRY: I'm thinking of calling it "Skunkweed."

RAINBOW: Really?

JERRY: No.

BONER: I got your email off your business card, dude, I'm gonna stay in touch.

RAINBOW: I don't think that's happening now, Boner.

BONER: If you need me to, I can fly out. I got frequent flyer miles.

RAINBOW: Boner, c'mon. Bye, Jerry.

BONER: Ciao, Jer.

(Boner and Rainbow leave. Christine returns with the baby.)

CHET: All set. We move.

CHRISTINE: Jerry, I sincerely hope things work out for you.

(She holds out her hand. Jerry takes it. They shake.)

JERRY: Hey, me, too.

(Chet opens the door.)

Um, Christine?

CHRISTINE: Yes, Jerry?

JERRY: Would you, um, tell Jo-Ellen for me, that, umm, I'm really sorry about . . . well, I'm not exactly sure what I'm sorry about, but I'm sorry. She's a really nice person and . . . um . . . I'm sorry.

CHRISTINE: That's really sweet. I'll tell her. *(She leaves)*

(Chet points at Jerry, starts to say something, but doesn't. He slams the door.

Jerry is left alone. He's not feeling good at all. He forces himself to pull it together: throws off the robe, goes into the bedroom.

His cell phone starts to ring. He comes out of the bedroom, buttoning his shirt.)

JERRY *(Into phone)*: Yeah? Oh, hi, honey. [. . .] Nothing, just, you know, working. How're the kids? Really? That's nice.

[. . .] Huh? No, just, you know, tired. [. . .] Yeah. Yeah. Laura? Oh, is that another call coming in? [. . .] No, I'll hold. I'm holding.

(Jerry puts his wallet back together. He looks at the pictures of his kids, then puts them away.)

Hi. [. . .] Oh, yeah, well you should go then. Say hi to her for me. [. . .] Yeah. And uh . . . Laura?

Can I just say something? Uh . . . I miss you. [. . .] No, no. That's it. No ulterior motive [. . .] NO! Now see you go right to that. I'm just here. Existing. And I just wanted you to know that I . . . can't wait to get home. [. . .]

(There is a knock on the door.

Jerry opens the door, still on the phone. Jo-Ellen is standing there. He holds up one finger to say "one sec.")

(Into phone) So OK. And . . . *(Fast)* Oh . . . and I needed some cash to, uh, pay for the rental car bill because the charge card I normally use is expired, and anyway . . . *(Jo-Ellen wanders in, a bit stiffly)* . . . I took a bunch of cash out of the checking account, so you probably shouldn't use it until tomorrow. OK? *(Slows down again)* OK. All right [. . .] I do. *(Hesitates)* I love you, too. Bye. *(He hangs up)*

(Cool) Hi.

JO-ELLEN: I just came up for a minute.

JERRY: I'm glad you did.

JO-ELLEN: Was that your wife?

JERRY: Yeah.

JO-ELLEN: You shouldn't get off the phone just because I'm here.

JERRY: No, no. She had another call coming in . . .

JO-ELLEN: Your kids are cute. I feel bad now I called her a bitch.

JERRY: It's OK. What she doesn't know won't hurt her.

(Beat.)

JO-ELLEN: Won't it?

JERRY: Jo-Ellen, ummmm . . . *(At a loss for words)*

JO-ELLEN: I know, I feel the same way.

JERRY: I am married.

JO-ELLEN: I know. You told me last night.

JERRY: And besides . . .

JO-ELLEN: Hey, you have this glamorous life. I'm just a girl from Volusia County. I'm ten years younger than you. I shouldn't expect anything. Should I?

JERRY: Well, actually, you should. But, um, unfortunately, if you do, your expectations will not bear fruit.

JO-ELLEN: Yeah. That's what I thought.

JERRY: I hope you're getting some of that thousand bucks.

JO-ELLEN: Oh, didn't Chet tell you? He decided not to take any money.

JERRY: He decided . . . what?

JO-ELLEN: Chet's got a felony record and it's stealin' no matter what you call it. If he got caught, he'd do time.

JERRY: Oh, and I thought he was being altruistic.

JO-ELLEN: He was. It was wrong. He knew it. My brother's really a nice guy. Deep down, once you get to know him.

(Jo-Ellen can't meet Jerry's eyes.)

JERRY *(Taking in her shyness)*: Listen. I . . .

JO-ELLEN: No. Wait. I gotta talk.

JERRY: OK.

JO-ELLEN: Remember last night, when we were sitting on the couch? And you told me about Nicole? How much you loved her. Do you remember what I said?

JERRY: Not really.

JO-ELLEN: Oh. OK. Then it doesn't make any difference.

JERRY: You said, you'd never been in love.

(Beat. Jo-Ellen's deeply pleased that he remembers. Now she can look at him.)

JO-ELLEN: That's right. That is what I said. Well, today . . . I wouldn't be able to say that. Because it wouldn't be true anymore.

JERRY: Wow.

JO-ELLEN: No. Listen. This isn't about you. It really isn't.

JERRY: I feel like such a creep.

JO-ELLEN: But you're not.

JERRY: I should have . . .

JO-ELLEN: No. That's not true . . . Jerry, if it'll make you feel any better. When I got in your car with you last night, in front of the motel, I knew what was happening. I knew what you were thinking. I knew you thought I was a prostitute. But I really wanted to see your hotel room. And have sex with you. Just to do it. For the kick.

JERRY: Oh.

JO-ELLEN: Ever hear that song, "Fooled Around and Fell in Love"? That's what happened. And I'm glad it happened. Even if I never see you again. Because now I know it *can* happen. Look, you're not the only Jerry in the world. Even though it kinda feels like that right now. There's got to be somebody else out there with a sense of humor and sweet brown eyes.

JERRY: Yeah, we . . . uh . . . have a lot of brown eyes in L.A.

JO-ELLEN: Uh-huh.

JERRY: A lot of Jerrys.

JO-ELLEN *(Smiling at his joke)*: So, see? Who's the bad guy?

(Beat as Jerry digests this.)

JERRY: Me. Still me.

JO-ELLEN: Well, me, too.

JERRY: Maybe it's possible to fall in love with someone a little bit, maybe just for the moment and um, if you're very, very careful, the love doesn't get, um, forgotten, and it turns into something you can cherish, in your heart, in a corner of your heart?

JO-ELLEN: I'd like to think that.

JERRY: Me, too.

JO-ELLEN: That's good. That's why I came up. I wouldn't want to say good-bye on a sour note. That would spoil everything.

JERRY: It would. *(Beat)* Laura's a bitch, because I make her into a bitch. That was all me. Pretty fucked-up. Laura and I are married. We have kids. We have a life. And I just figured that out. Today.

JO-ELLEN: You're very lucky.

JERRY: Yeah, isn't that funny?

JO-ELLEN: Not funny. Good.

(Beat.)

JERRY: Hey.

(They hug.)

JO-ELLEN *(Brisk, so she doesn't cry)*: OK! Gotta go. Chet gave me five minutes and then he said he was coming up to get me.

JERRY: Don't want that. Please. I don't need any more Chet today.

JO-ELLEN: No.

(They laugh. Another hug.)

Bye.

(She leaves. Jerry closes the door. He sits on the couch and turns on the TV.)

TV VOICE-OVER: Dr. Phil, the problem is, we just don't love each other anymore. I mean, we love each other, but we don't *like* each other. And it's hard to live with someone you don't like.

(Blackout.)

END OF PLAY

SKUNKWEED

ERIC BOGOSIAN has starred in a wide variety of film, TV and stage roles. Most recently, he created the character Captain Danny Ross on the long-running series *Law & Order: Criminal Intent*, and starred on Broadway with Laura Linney in Donald Margulies's *Time Stands Still*.

His celebrated work, *Talk Radio*, which he wrote and in which he starred, premiered at the New York Shakespeare Festival in 1987, was adapted to film by director Oliver Stone in 1988, and premiered on Broadway in 2007, in a production starring Liev Schreiber. *Talk Radio* was a Pulitzer Prize finalist, and in 1988 Bogosian was awarded the Berlin Film Festival's Silver Bear for his work on the film.

Bogosian's other plays and solo work include *subUrbia* (Lincoln Center Theater, 1994; adapted to film by director Richard Linklater, 1996); *Sex, Drugs, Rock & Roll; Pounding Nails in the Floor with My Forehead; Griller; Humpty Dumpty; Wake Up and Smell the Coffee; Drinking in America* and *Notes from Underground*. He has received three Obie Awards and a Drama Desk Award. *100*, a collection of monologues, commemorating thirty years of his solo-performance career, will be published by TCG in 2013.

Bogosian is the author of three novels: *Mall, Wasted Beauty* and *Perforated Heart*. The film adaptation of *Mall* is in post-production.

For the last five years, Bogosian has been researching a non-fiction work on the "Nemesis" assassins, a secret organization of Armenian nationals who succeeded in assassinating the Turkish leadership responsible for the Armenian genocide.

He is married to director Jo Bonney and lives in New York City.